Buyer Power and Competition in European Food Retailing

For Jan, Cath, Ratula and Sally

Buyer Power and Competition in European Food Retailing

Roger Clarke

Professor of Microeconomics, Cardiff University, UK

Stephen Davies

Professor of Economics, University of East Anglia, UK

Paul Dobson

Professor of Retail Strategy and Industrial Organization, Loughborough University, UK

Michael Waterson

Professor of Economics, University of Warwick, UK

Edward Elgar

Cheltenham UK • Northampton, MA, USA

Published by
Edward Elgar Publishing Limited
Glensanda House
Montpellier Parade
Cheltenham
Glos GL50 1UA
UK

Edward Elgar Publishing, Inc.
136 West Street
Suite 202
Northampton
Massachusetts 01060
USA

A catalogue record for this book is available from the British Library

Library of Congress Cataloging in Publication Data

Buyer power and competition in European food retailing /
Roger Clarke ... [et al.].
  p.cm.
Includes bibliographical references (p.) and index.
  1. Food industry and trade–European Union countries.
  2. Grocery trade–European Union countries. 3. Retail trade
  –European Union countries. I. Clarke, Roger.

HD9015.A2 B89 2002
381'.456413'094—dc21   2002017910

ISBN 1-84064-685-3
Printed and bound in Great Britain by MPG Books Ltd, Bodmin, Cornwall

Contents

Figures

Tables

viii   *Buyer Power and Competition in European Food Retailing*

Preface

Recent years have seen a tremendous change in the food retailing landscape across the European Union. Less than twenty years ago food retailing was dominated by many small or medium-sized firms, but since then large supermarket and hypermarket chains have emerged to dominate the retail scene in most EU countries. One view of this would be that consumers have benefited from these developments because larger stores (owned by these groups) offer more product choice (under more convenient conditions), and the large chains can use their bulk buying power to obtain lower prices from suppliers which they then pass on to consumers. And there is clearly merit in this view.

At the same time, however, as these groups become larger there is concern that they will be better able to exert their market power over both suppliers and consumers if retail competition is restricted or distorted in their favour. In purchasing, they may not only use their market power to extract lower prices from suppliers but also possibly engage in anti-competitive behaviour (e.g. in boycotting suppliers, restricting sources of supply for smaller or new retailers, or imposing unfair charges on suppliers). In the retail market, they may fail to pass cost savings on to consumers so that prices are not as low as they might otherwise be with more intense and varied retail competition. Moreover, since the consolidation process seems presently relentless in many countries there is a real need to consider what additional competition problems are likely to emerge in the future and whether action is required now. This could conceivably be in the form of tightening merger policy and stronger attempts to prevent major retailers using anti-competitive practices. These and other policy issues, such as possible changes to planning and zoning laws and the extension of laws to protect small suppliers, are presently being hotly debated.

As yet, no clear consensus has emerged on the scale of the problem and what appropriate action, if any, should be undertaken. It is against this backdrop that this book should be viewed. It reports work undertaken, in particular, on buying power originally conducted for the European Commission under Study Contract IV/98/ETD/078. In this work, we examined theoretical and policy issues relevant to buyer power in food retailing, statistical evidence on the structure of food retailing in the EU, and conducted a number of case studies of food retailing in major EU countries. The results of this study are reported here.

We provide evidence of the rapid growth in concentration (both on the buying and supplying side) in most EU countries, and show, in the case studies, its practical effect. The study also discusses policy action already undertaken to curb supermarket group buyer (and seller) power within some EU countries, and considers whether further action is (or is likely to be) required.

In undertaking this book there are a number of people that we owe special thanks to. First, there are our country study contributors: Marie-Laure Allain and Claire Chambolle for France, Christoph Schenk for Germany, and Juan Manez Castillejo for Spain and the UK, for their work on the case studies, and for undertaking the interviews on which the material in Part III is based. We would also like to thank the European Commission for giving permission to publish this book, and Jorma Pihlatie, in particular, for his comments and advice during much of the original project for DG Competition. We are most grateful to the representatives of the many companies and organisations that provided us with information and gave interviews and we have respected their requests not to report any commercially sensitive material supplied to us. Finally, we would like to thank Barry Hogan at Cardiff University who re-typed and undertook some of the formatting of the book.

Roger Clarke
Steve Davies
Paul Dobson
Mike Waterson

April 2002

1. Introduction

The last couple of decades have witnessed considerable changes in retailing across most developed countries with the emergence of new store formats, the increased prevalence of retail chains, the development of out-of-town and edge-of-town retail parks, and significant investment in new technology (such as Electronic Point of Sale) and improved logistics. At the same time, the sector has seen the rise of giant corporations controlling significant proportions of overall domestic retail sales, and the emergence of internationally operating retail groups. The size of these retailers now ranks them among the largest companies in their country of origin. For instance, the largest Belgian company, Delhaize 'Le Lion', is a retailer, Britain's Tesco and J. Sainsbury both appear in the UK top 20 companies; Germany has the giant Metro group; and Wal-Mart Stores is the second largest company in the world, with turnover of US$ 193 bn and 1,244,000 employees (*Fortune*, 3 September 2001).[1]

Among all the areas of retailing, it is food retailing which stands out as having seen the most profound changes, and where, by its sheer size and importance, the developments have had the greatest impact on consumers. Here, along with the trend towards large store formats carrying as many as 20,000 product lines, there has been considerable consolidation at both the national level and for Europe as a whole. For instance, the top ten grocers in Europe accounted for 27.8 per cent of the market in 1992, but 36.2 per cent of the European market in 1997, according to the retail analysts M+M Eurodata.[2] Moreover, while increased retail concentration has been a feature of developed countries around the world, it is notable that ranked in terms of world revenue in food retailing the top three places in the *Fortune* list are taken by European retailers – Carrefour of France, and Metro and Rewe of Germany – raising the prospect that such large firms may be able to command market power over suppliers and consumers alike and earn super-normal profits as a result.[3]

Potentially then, retailer power is an important issue in Europe. The subject featured strongly in the European Commission's Green Paper on Vertical Restraints, released in January 1997. It has arisen in the context of investigations into merger proposals, for example the proposed consolidation of Finland's two largest food retail groups (Kesko/Tuko).[4] Also, at the national level, retailer power is seen to be of concern and the subject of inquiries by competition authorities – for example, in the UK, the Competition Commission has recently investigated the

1

leading food retailers producing its report in October 2000. Moreover, the issue is likely to remain to the fore, given the tendency for consolidation through merger and concern over market practices including vertical arrangements with suppliers.

However, while all European countries have experienced considerable changes in the food retailing sector, there are substantial differences in the structure across different countries and as a result different policy issues arise. In some countries, like the UK, a limited number of integrated store groups control over 50 per cent of the market and as a consequence both the buying and selling sides of the market tend to be concentrated. In other countries, buyer groups representing (technically) independent retailers (e.g. as 'voluntary chains') are prevalent with the consequence that at the national level the buyer-side of the market is more concentrated than the seller-side. This feature is quite common in Europe where buyer groups can be the leading food buying organisations – for instance, Germany's Markant Handels is the largest food buyer by turnover, Spain's large purchasing groups, Euromadi and IFA Espanola, are ranked numbers one and two, and France's Intermarché is, again, the largest in the country in terms of turnover. In some countries, like Greece and Italy, the market remains relatively unconcentrated on both the buying and selling side and independent retailers remain dominant.

1.1 THEORETICAL BACKGROUND

This study is specifically concerned with the buyer power of retailers and thus the form, nature and behaviour of them as buyers takes on considerable importance. Here buyer power arises from the ability of retail firms to obtain from suppliers more favourable terms than those available to other buyers or would otherwise be expected under normal competitive conditions. Apart from the ability to extract discounts on transactions from suppliers, buyer power may manifest itself in the contractual obligations (as vertical restraints) which retailers may be able to place on suppliers. These could take a number of forms, such as listing charges (where buyers require payment of a fee before goods are purchased from the listed supplier), slotting allowances (where fees are charged for store shelf-space allocation), retroactive discounts on goods already sold, buyer-forced application of most favoured nation (MFN) clauses (with contractual obligations for the supplier not to sell to another retailer at a lower price), unjustified high contributions to retailer promotional expenses, and insistence on exclusive supply.

Buyer power may exist in isolation – where the selling power of retailers is limited by intense competition. This might be the case, for example, where retailing is highly fragmented on the selling side but co-ordinated (through buyer groups) on the buying side. But often it might be that the buyer power of retailers is linked with their selling power, where one power reinforces the other, and thus the effects of one on the other and their combined influence on economic welfare take on some importance.

1.2 WELFARE TRADE-OFFS

In regard to public policy, the buyer power of retailers is not a new concern for competition authorities. Yet the policy treatment clearly remains a contentious area of competition policy. In the United States, the growth in mass retailing in the 1930s prompted the Robinson-Patman Act, which sought to prohibit suppliers from offering preferential terms to selected buyers. Buyer power was then viewed as threatening the competitive structure of retail markets. Yet this legislation has received considerable criticism for serving to impede the competitive process and development of efficient forms of distribution. In contrast most other countries have not adopted similar *per se* rules, but instead have chosen to rely on a rule-of-reason (case-by-case) approach. However, whether there should be a general presumption in favour or against buyer power in this approach is far from clear, and different countries have in practice taken different stances. Nevertheless, the continued consolidation of the retailing sector has brought the issue to the fore, where there is growing concern that the buying power of retailers may have adverse economic effects on the viability and efficiency of suppliers and also, as noted above, that such power may go hand-in-hand with increased selling power and thus potentially have adverse effects on consumer welfare.

Nevertheless, while it is recognised that retail concentration, particularly in the grocery sector, has risen sharply in recent years, it may be argued that this can be socially beneficial where it results in buyer power which can be used to counter the market power of manufacturers. Here, the exercise of this power prevents manufacturers from exploiting their position as fully as they could if they were faced with a less concentrated retail sector. Then, if buyer power could exist among retailers without those retailers having significant market power of their own, it is possible that buyer power could lead to lower wholesale prices which, as a result of effective retailer competition, would be passed on to consumers in lower final prices. Lower final prices would mean higher output and higher welfare.

The contrary view to this benign picture is that buyer power may ultimately damage economic welfare. Although it may lead to lower prices in the short run, there may be longer term detrimental effects resulting from buyer power. In the context of retail grocery markets the effects may be to force manufacturers to reduce investment in new products or product improvements, advertising and brand building. It could eliminate secondary brands and weaken primary brands while strengthening the position of private label (store) brands, and in the process cause wholesale prices to smaller retailers to rise, further weakening them as competitors. In other words, buyer power may have the effect of distorting retail and producer competition.

The fear is that ultimately competition in food retailing could be between a small number of fully integrated retailers. This could mean that they extract high rents and possibly set high prices depending on the nature of competition between them.

Given these two sets of opposing arguments, it is clear that evaluation of buyer power may therefore involve a series of trade-offs. The first trade-off is exclusively short run between increased buyer power and increased retailer market power. Specifically, if two retailers merge they may have more buyer power which can be used to put downward pressure on wholesale prices, but they may also have more market power which can be used to raise rather than lower final prices. If the latter outweighs the former, prices may rise to the detriment of consumers and economic welfare generally.

The second trade-off is between the short run benefits of lower prices and the longer term effects of competition noted above.

Given such trade-offs, it is not clear a priori what will be the net economic welfare effect of buyer power – but this can be expected to vary according to market conditions and other factors, lending support to the argument in favour of a case-by-case policy approach. In this regard, insights gained from economic theory may prove useful in providing some policy guidance into the conditions for which buyer power may be socially benign or, in contrast, be deleterious to economic welfare.

1.3 PLAN OF THE BOOK

The rest of the book is organised as follows. Part I examines theoretical and policy underpinnings. We begin, in Chapter 2, by reviewing and analysing the economic theory of buyer power as our starting point. From this analysis we put forward, in Chapter 3, a set of buyer power propositions and a structured framework for considering the net welfare effects of buyer power. Further, the term 'buyer power' itself has been the subject of much debate. Its definition is considered in Chapter 4, along with its economic measurement and definition of the relevant market. This is then followed in Chapter 5 by a brief commentary on present competition policy and law towards buyer power.

Part II of the book moves on from theoretical and policy analysis to consider the actual structure and nature of food retail distribution in Europe. It presents a formal statistical analysis of food retailing across the European Union, providing a bridge between the theoretical discussion of Part I and the case studies of Part III. Thus, one purpose is to quantify some of the concepts, like buyer and seller concentration featured in the discussion in Part I, for the EU retail food sector –

both for individual member states and for the EU in aggregate. In addition, it provides a backcloth for the more in-depth case study analysis which focuses on specific countries developed in subsequent chapters. Part II includes two chapters. The first, Chapter 6, draws on existing statistical sources to build up a picture of the key structural dimensions of the sector. Chapter 7 takes the statistical analysis further by constructing an entirely new database – the EU Retail Food Market Share Matrix – which is designed to yield an integrated, and internally consistent, statistical mapping of the structure of the sector at both the aggregate EU and national levels, and for the leading firms therein. This provides additional insights on some elements of structure, such as aggregate EU concentration and cross-border operations, while improving the quality of information on others, e.g. measures of concentration at the national level. It also provides background information of relevance to our selection of case studies in Part III.

Part III of the book provides case analysis from four countries – France, Germany, Spain and the United Kingdom – which considers for each country the characteristics and evolution of market structure, competition in food retailing, retailer and buying group buying power, own-label development, and any other special market features. Each of the country reports also contains specific information on the production and distribution of three representative product groups – washing powders, coffee (instant and roast and ground), and butter and non-butter spreads (margarine) – as illustrations of the nature of supply and buyer activity in the sector. The four cases are discussed in successive chapters (8–11) and our conclusions from the cases, both in terms of cross-country comparisons and product comparisons, are provided in a summary chapter (12).

Chapter 13 concludes the book, taking account of the results and conclusions of the three parts of our analysis to draw some general conclusions about the state of competition and the extent and effects of buyer power in the food retail distribution sector of the European Union. This chapter also focuses on policy issues and future issues that competition policy authorities are likely to face.

NOTES

1. All figures relate to rankings by revenue.
2. Press release (8 August 1998) – see http://www.mm-eurodata.de.
3. It should be noted that Wal-Mart Stores, even though much of its sales come from food retailing, is classified by *Fortune* as a general merchandiser. In this category Britain's Marks & Spencer has, until recently, been ranked number one in terms of profitability. Interestingly, the most profitable major food retailer in terms of profit generated as a proportion of revenue is also a British company – Asda group.
4. Kesko/Tuko, case IV/M.784 (OJEC L1 10, 26 April 1997).

PART I: THEORETICAL AND POLICY UNDERPINNINGS

In this part we develop the relevant theoretical material needed for an examination of buyer power in Chapter 2. This covers basic models and a more advanced treatment of the subject, not typically dealt with in intermediate microeconomics texts. This leads onto a set of 'buyer power propositions' in Chapter 3. We see that even commonly held views, such as 'buyer power is desirable' must be carefully treated and subjected to caveats. Arising out of these propositions we have one of the central elements of the book, a proposed framework for the analysis of buyer power in a public policy context. This feeds closely into the later analysis, particularly our case studies of particular markets, where it guides us in our assessment of the empirical findings.

It is a commonly held view that to examine something, one must be able to measure it. Therefore in Chapter 4 we exposit and develop measures of buyer power, leading to our outlining a set of practical procedures which might be used in assessing whether buyer power is a significant problem, worthy of more detailed investigation, in particular cases which may arise. We also tackle the question of market definition in the context of a relevant market on the buying side, drawing on the Commission's Notice on Market Definition on the selling side.

Chapter 5 concludes this part of the book with a discussion of public policy towards retail buyer power in Europe. It highlights some of the different approaches taken across member states in the EU with regard to the exploitation of power by dominant buyers, the effects of the economic dependence of suppliers on retailers, and the policy treatment of retailer associations.

2. The Economics of Monopsony and Buyer Bargaining Power

The analysis of monopsony (where a single buyer faces competitive suppliers) and bilateral monopoly (where a single buyer faces a single supplier) is extensively covered in standard microeconomics textbooks. However, rarely is consideration given to more general market forms involving buyer power and the related empirical and legal questions. One source which does deal extensively with these issues is Blair and Harrison (1993), which seeks to address the economic theory of buyer power and relates this to relevant competition law cases (at least as applied in the United States). This source is quite comprehensive in its treatment of monopsony, dominant buyer firms, buyer cartels, and bilateral monopoly, yet does not cover more complicated bargaining situations, nor does it discuss empirical and, more specifically, econometric studies.

The summary analysis contained in Dobson, Waterson and Chu (1998) is intended to give broad, but less detailed, coverage of the economic issues – setting out the basic economics of unilateral and bilateral market power as a basis for developing a policy framework for examining buyer power. Given the relevance to the present book, we draw directly on this analysis to illustrate the key arguments. This analysis will prove useful for the general insights it provides and as a basis for our specific buyer power propositions, which are set out in the next chapter. The focus here is on price and quantity effects arising from the exercise of buyer power and possible anti-competitive practices. The approach uses standard comparative static analysis and then provides supplementary comments on dynamic aspects.

We begin with the case of unilateral market power, where there is at most imperfect competition on the buyer side but perfect competition on the supplier side. We then move on to discuss bilateral market power where competition is limited on both sides of the market. Finally we consider possible anti-competitive practices.

2.1 MONOPSONY

The most straightforward case of buyer power is that of a single buyer facing (perfectly) competitive sellers – so-called 'pure monopsony'. The economic analysis of this case is directly analogous to that of pure monopoly (where a single seller faces competitive buyers). As such, the welfare implications arising from their exercise of market power are illustrated in a similar fashion. We begin by demonstrating the standard textbook treatment of monopsony, before developing the discussion to cover oligopsony and related market structures where buyers operate in imperfectly competitive conditions (so still may be able to exercise market power) while sellers are perfectly competitive (and thus have no corresponding market power).

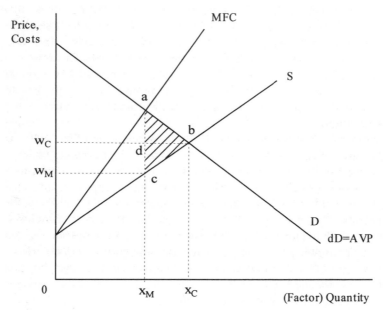

Figure 2.1 Monopsony welfare losses

For base reference, consider the situation of a competitive (supplying) industry which faces familiar demand and supply curves, D and S as represented in Figure 2.1. The competitive equilibrium is where D and S intersect, resulting in quantity x_C and price w_C. Now assume that we are dealing with an input market where the product is used by buyers in later stages of production, so that demand curve D represents the average revenue product obtained from the input which is later used to produce the finished product, referred to as the 'derived demand' for the input and denoted dD which is equal to average (net) value (revenue) product of the factor (AVP).

We can now consider the impact of a monopsonist's buying behaviour on market prices. Referring to the upward sloping supply curve S in Figure 2.1, as the (single) firm buys more units of the input, there needs to be a higher level of production to accommodate the increased demand, resulting in an increase in the unit cost of production. However, the increase in unit price needs to be paid not only for new production but also for existing levels of production.[1] Accordingly, each marginal unit costs more than the average cost, thus we are left with the marginal factor cost curve, denoted by MFC, which lies above the supply curve S. Suppose further that the (single) buyer is a price-taker in the downstream market – for example it is the archetypal monopsony employer in a 'one-mill town' which sells in a competitive product market. Its profit maximising output would then be determined by the intersection of its derived demand curve dD and its marginal factor cost curve MFC yielding equilibrium price w_M and quantity x_M. The associated welfare loss from this scenario is represented by the triangular region *abc*.

As Figure 2.1 illustrates, the monopsonist restricts purchases below the competitive level, so that from a social welfare perspective too few resources are employed (i.e. there are unrealised gains from further trade) resulting in an allocative welfare loss. As a consequence, the input price paid falls (below the competitive level), but as the monopsonist competes in a competitive output market, the going price (say, p^*) is unaffected by its purchasing behaviour. As a consequence, producer surplus declines by the area w_Cbcw_M, while purchaser surplus rises by the difference between the rectangle w_Cdcw_M and triangle *abd*, leaving deadweight social welfare loss as the area *abc*.

In the situation where the monopsonist is also a monopolist in the downstream market, for which Nichol (1943) uses the term 'monemporist' (i.e. a monopsonist-monopolist), there would be a downward-sloping derived demand for the input, along with a second curve, marginal to this derived demand curve, that reflects the marginal revenue product of the input, shown in Figure 2.2 as MRP.[2] The intersection of the MRP curve with that of MFC indicates the profit-maximising input quantity for the monemporist. Again, equilibrium levels of both purchase price (w_{MM}) and quantity (x_{MM}) in the input market are below the competitive equilibrium. In this situation, the welfare loss from exercising buyer power is compounded by the presence of seller power, with the additional welfare loss (due to seller power) represented by the region *abcd* in Figure 2.2.

Although this discussion is presented primarily in terms of a monopsonist, as the only buyer in the market, the principles are readily applicable to situations where some buyers (either singly or jointly) recognise their ability to influence

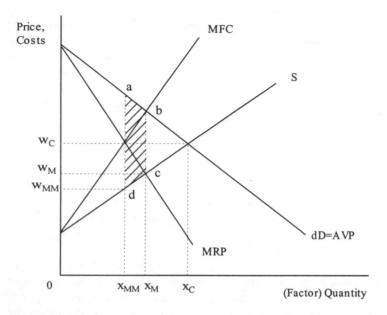

Figure 2.2 Additional welfare losses from monopsonist possessing monopoly power

market prices. In such instances, three conditions appear necessary for the exercise of buyer power: (i) the buyers contribute to a substantial portion of purchases in the market; (ii) there are barriers to entry into the buyer's market; and (iii) the supply curve is upward sloping. Under these circumstances it is straightforward to apply the principles of oligopoly theory to model situations of oligopsony where strategic interaction occurs between a few buyers competing in a market – see for example the seminal analysis of Stackelberg (1934) and Fellner (1949). Similarly, the dominant firm model (Forchheimer, 1908) can be readily applied for consideration of dominant buyer behaviour, where the leading firm faces a competitive fringe of other buyers, e.g. Blair and Harrison (1992, pp. 49–51) and Veendorp (1987).[3] For both extensions, the results translate directly. In the case of oligopsony, generally, the fewer the number of buyers the greater is the distortion in factor price and quantity below the competitive level, all other things being equal.[4] Similarly, in a dominant buyer framework, the greater the market control by the key buyer, in terms of its market share with respect to that of the competitive fringe, the greater is its ability to exert power to reduce price below the competitive level. Moreover, as a general result, applying to monopsony, oligopsony or a dominant buyer situation, it should be observed that, for a given (derived) demand curve, the lower the elasticity of supply the greater the deviation from competitive price.[5]

In the case of joint action by buyers, where they seek to maximise joint profits, the analysis corresponds directly to that of a cartel controlling sales. Buyer co-ordination to reduce factor prices by restricting collective purchases serves, *ceteris paribus*, to reduce social welfare, and the deadweight welfare loss is equivalent to that generated by a monopsonist, i.e. as shown in Figure 2.1.[6] The detrimental effect on welfare is compounded if collusion also spills over into the buyers' output market, with the result equivalent to the monopsonist-monopolist (monemporist) outcome illustrated in Figure 2.2.

Thus for a range of circumstances, we may conclude that buyer power exerted against competitive sellers is likely to have a detrimental welfare effect where it involves buyers acting singly or jointly to restrict purchases – where buyer surplus is increased but does not compensate (if surplus is equally weighted) for the loss in (supplier) producer surplus, resulting in foregone economic surplus.[7]

The question which naturally follows is how likely strong buyers are to find themselves in the position of being able to exploit an upward sloping supply function. For instance, it may be considered that many industries are characterised by constant or even increasing returns, and accordingly buyers may not face an upward sloping supply. However, an empirical study which has some bearing in this regard is that provided by Shea (1993), which found that for twenty six U.S. manufacturing industries studied, only three exhibited downward sloping supply functions, relating to prepared feeds, construction equipment, and aircraft. Of the rest, more than twice as many were upward sloping as were flat. Sixteen industries (such as lumber, drugs, paints, tires, stone, clay and glass, cement and electronic components) were found to have upward sloping supply functions, while seven other industries had flat supply functions (such as plumbing and heating products, floor coverings, and animal and marine fats and oils). Accordingly, the assumption of an upward sloping supply may actually have some broad empirical relevance, even to manufacturing industries where increasing returns might have been more commonly expected.[8] However, as yet there have been no equivalent studies on retail goods markets – e.g. examining supply conditions for manufactured final goods. Nevertheless, it is apparent for a number of agricultural markets that upward sloping supply may be a feature and consequently powerful retailers may be in a position to exploit buyer power if they deal directly with producers.

In summary, welfare is likely to be adversely affected by the exercise of monopsony power in conditions where buyers have the ability to exploit a competitive supplying industry to depress market prices below competitive levels. The associated welfare losses are due to reduced producer surplus, and unless the buyers have market power when selling their output, there is no direct effect on final consumers. However, where buyer and seller power are jointly held (e.g. by a monemporist) the outcome is likely to be allocatively inefficient and in particular the welfare of both factor producers and final consumers is likely to be adversely affected.

However, the conclusion that the exercise of monopsony power is socially detrimental needs to be qualified in terms of two important caveats. Firstly, there may be off-setting efficiency benefits. The market may, for example, be a 'natural' monopsony where productive efficiency requires that there be a single buyer of an input and thus a welfare trade-off results, analogous to that of monopoly (e.g. Williamson, 1968), involving productive gains but allocative deadweight welfare loss. For example, network economies may be present in purchasing and collecting, e.g. in agricultural markets such as for milk, implying that the activity is most efficiently undertaken by a single firm but such a firm may then have monopsony power. In the context of retailing, logistical economies may yield similar benefits. Similarly, with a buyer cartel there may be cost-savings from joint purchasing behaviour, e.g. regarding reduced transaction costs or achieving economies of scale in production and warehousing, and other efficiency benefits (e.g. Mathewson and Winter, 1996). This argument is particularly strong in the context of retailing where purchasing groups have become increasingly common – with competition authorities and courts recognising the efficiency benefits that these organisations may offer.[9] Secondly, it should be apparent from examination of Figure 2.1, for example, that if the monopsonist could practice (first degree) price discrimination in making its purchases, i.e. pay each unit its exact cost of production rather than setting just a single market price, then the purchaser can obtain the entire economic surplus which would be generated under competitive market conditions (thus eradicating any deadweight welfare loss in the factor market).

As a final point, it should be noted that the above discussion has been cast in terms of static welfare considerations. In addition, attention needs to be given to possible dynamic effects and here concern is often expressed about possible detrimental welfare effects arising from the damage to the long term viability of producers resulting from the exercise of monopsony power. This can have an economic impact when, for example, buyer power reduces prices for suppliers, and thus their income, making it difficult for them to finance required investments, which might then be postponed or even foregone completely. Similarly, suppliers may be reluctant to undertake investments when they anticipate (post-contractual) opportunistic behaviour by powerful buyers seeking to exploit supplier commitments. In both cases, supplier efficiency may suffer which might ultimately feed through to higher prices for consumers than would otherwise be the case. These points touch on the welfare problems which may arise from economic dependency, where an agent (a supplier) relies on a powerful principal (a buyer) for its economic survival when it has aligned its production to meet exclusively the needs of the buyer, and whereby it has cut off the possibility of supplying other buyers (at least in the short run).

2.2 BILATERAL MARKET POWER

Thus far, we have considered the exercise of monopsony power against competitive suppliers. Matters become more complicated in markets where seller power is also present on the other side of the market. Analysis of this situation has focused primarily on the case of 'bilateral monopoly', where an upstream monopolist is the sole producer of a factor required uniquely by a downstream monopolist in undertaking its production.

Figure 2.3 presents the standard diagrammatic treatment of bilateral monopoly where a monopoly producer of a factor trades with a monopsony purchaser (e.g. Bowley (1928) and Morgan (1949)). If the buyer acted in a perfectly competitive manner in its output market, the derived demand for the input would equal average (net) value product of the factor, represented by the curve AVP = D_C.[10] However, if the monopsonist buyer acts as a monopolist in its output market then the derived demand for the factor will be MRP, the curve marginal to AVP. As in the previous section, MRP is the marginal revenue product of the factor, that is the additional revenue obtained from employing an additional unit of the factor. The curve labelled MMRP is marginal to MRP, and represents the marginal revenue associated with selling the factor to a buyer which has monopoly power but no monopsony power. The curve AC denotes the seller's average cost for producing the good, and MC its marginal cost. If the seller behaved as a perfect competitor, then MC represents its supply curve, S_C. Finally, the curve MFC is marginal to MC, and, as before, indicates the marginal factor cost of the input to a monopsonist buyer, treating the seller as having no market power.

Let us first note the non-cooperative solutions which would arise if only one party held market power and sets price to which the other party simply responds by determining the quantity. In the monopoly outcome, the seller dominates and sets price and the buyer responds by purchasing in a competitive manner. In this case, the seller equates MC with MMRP, with the result that quantity would be x_S and price w_S. On the other hand, in the monopsony outcome, the buyer dominates and sets price leaving the seller to determine the output level. If the buyer also acts as a monopolist in its output market then it equates MRP with MFC, resulting in quantity x_B and price w_B.

However, with both firms recognising their mutual interdependence and with neither side being in a position to impose a price and let the other respond by determining quantity, we may expect both parties to agree on setting quantity at a level which maximises their joint profits (i.e. is Pareto optimal from their joint perspective) and then divide the spoils through bargaining over the trading price. In this case, the quantity would be x^*, where MC is equal to MRP. In terms of the price at which the two parties would trade, we can note that this could be so high as to leave the buyer with zero profit from the transaction, i.e. when the price equals the buyer's average value product at point H in Figure 2.3. Alternatively, it could be so low as to equal the seller's average cost of producing its output, at point L, in which case the seller derives no profit from the transaction. Which point on the contract curve (i.e. the line between H and L) would be chosen depends upon the outcome of a bargain between the two agents.[11]

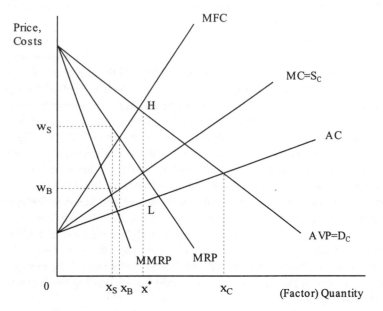

Figure 2.3 Bilateral monopoly

As shown in Figure 2.3, the joint-profit-maximising level, x^*, is higher than both x_S and x_B.[12] In some sense, then, with agreement on this level, there is a social welfare gain from having opposing selling and buying power compared to power existing on only one side of the market. However, it should be pointed out that while x^* is Pareto optimal from the firms' perspective in maximising joint profits, it is not implied that social efficiency is accordingly maximised. For example, when the buyer is a monopolist in its output market, joint profits are maximised when the buyer uses its monopoly power and quantity is restricted below the competitive level. Indeed, it can be observed that the firms are able to earn profits up to the point which corresponds with the intersection of AVP and AC, i.e. x_C. Nevertheless, the analysis does indicate that the welfare consequences of bilateral market power may be less severe than the cases where market power is unopposed. For example, the level x_S corresponds *mutatis mutandis* to 'successive monopoly' where an upstream monopolist sets price to a downstream monopolist, which in turn takes this price as parametric and treats it as a cost level when determining its own output price. Alternatively, the level x_B corresponds to the 'monempory' (i.e. monopsony-monopoly) solution whereby the firm exercises both (unopposed) monopsony and monopoly power.

An obvious extension is to consider the case where the buyer has monopsony power, but no monopoly power in the final market. An example of this might be a buyer alliance which is united for the purposes of negotiating but whose firms compete independently as sellers. In this case, AVP becomes the relevant base curve on the demand side, with MRP becoming the marginal curve. Negotiation in the bilateral monopoly situation would then be over the transaction price for the quantity corresponding to the intersection of AVP and MC, i.e. a quantity exceeding that of x^* and thus socially preferable. An interpretation would be that, for all other things equal, a buyer alliance with members competing as sellers would offer a higher level of societal welfare than a single buying firm which also had monopoly power on the selling side. In the context of food retailing, this suggests that buyer groups may be of less welfare concern (where group members compete against each other in the retail market) than store groups which have both buying and selling power.

Beyond bilateral monopoly, we could consider market structures with more than one firm on either side of the market. For instance, Dobson and Waterson (1997) develop an analysis based on a (single) supplier bargaining with (differentiated) oligopolistic retailers and examine the effects of increased consolidation in the retail sector on consumer prices and economic welfare. Here there are two opposing forces. On the one hand, consolidation may increase retailers' power over the supplier sufficiently to reduce transfer prices, which can feed through to lower final prices when there is intense competition in the retail market. On the other hand, retailer consolidation can lead to increased selling power at this level which may allow retailers increased margins, tending to undermine their bargaining strength given their greater ability to afford bargaining concessions with the consequence that transfer prices may not be significantly reduced and as a result higher final prices may ensue. Which effect dominates is shown to depend greatly on the intensity of retail competition – the former effect is stronger when competition is intense, otherwise the latter effect dominates and consolidation leads to higher prices for consumers.

2.3 ANTI-COMPETITIVE PRACTICES

In addition to the price effects noted above, buyer (or seller) power can give rise to possible anti-competitive effects. These take the form, typically, of vertical restraints where one side of a bargaining relation (here, the supermarket chains) imposes terms and conditions on the other side. It is usually argued that, in the absence of market power, vertical restraints are benign, either having no effect on competition or producing efficiency gains (see, for example, Bork, 1978). If there is market power, however, such conditions could have the effect of extending market power, and dampening competition, and policy action may, therefore, be required.

This issue is particularly important in food retail distribution because supermarket chains in many 'northern' EU countries have large (and growing) market shares, and tend to impose a variety of terms and conditions on suppliers. In some cases, these are likely to be benign; for example, many supermarket chains require suppliers to deliver to distribution centres rather than directly to stores, as this enables them to minimise distribution costs. On the other hand, if supermarket chains create dependency relations with suppliers, whereby the latter supply all their output to just one store (or chain), there may be more cause for concern.

Most supermarket chains in the EU (and the US) use similar vertical restraints. The most common types are:

- listing fees, required by supermarket chains to list (i.e. stock) a product;
- slotting allowances, required to position a product on a particular shelf or end-of-aisle display;
- retrospective payments, required at the end of the year and linked to the value of sales of the product in that year;
- special payments, required to support a new store opening or refurbishment;
- long payment terms, whereby supermarket chains can delay payment of invoices and, effectively, obtain free loans;
- product boycotts, whereby supermarket chains refuse to stock the products of a particular producer.

To some extent, especially where supermarket chains face large, oligopolistic suppliers, these practices can be seen as part of the bargaining process, and they may not have effects on economic efficiency itself, conventionally defined. However, the existence of market power can give rise to abuse and has, in fact, led to a number of countries in the EU seeking to curb that abuse. Special consideration has been given to retrospective payments, in the case where these are imposed unilaterally, special payments, especially where imposed unilaterally, again, and long payment terms. All have been seen, at least in some jurisdictions, as issues of policy concern against which action has been taken. The ability of supermarket chains to boycott suppliers and thereby deny them access to (part of) the consumer market is also an issue, and boycotts have, in fact, occurred.

Supermarket buying power can be seen to be a problem, especially where smaller suppliers are concerned. Small suppliers of own brands or secondary products will be under considerable pressure to reduce their prices, and may not be able to make an adequate return. They may be required to fulfil certain conditions, e.g. supply to a particular distribution centre, which reduces the costs of supermarket chains but imposes a significant cost on them. And if they are dependent on one or a group of stores, or one particular chain (as, for example, but not exclusively, producers of fresh produce), they may have to accept lower prices, or certain terms and conditions, rather than lose all their sales.

The presence of market power on the buying side can, therefore, give rise to ancillary problems, as our discussion later in the book will show.

NOTES

1. The assumption is that compensation for higher unit costs of production can be obtained for all levels of sales. Specifically, price discrimination is ruled out, for example, because of arbitrage activities.
2. MRP is defined as the revenue obtained from the purchase of an additional unit of the input. The MRP curve necessarily lies below the downward-sloping demand curve dD because the additional revenue generated by each marginal unit reduces the average revenue product on all units sold.
3. Equally, one could also adapt the dominant cartel model, developed by Saving (1970), to analyse the situation where a colluding group of buyers compete with a competitive fringe of other buyers.
4. The notable exception is where (symmetric) oligopsonists compete on price setting for a homogeneous input. In this case, the result is analogous to Bertrand oligopoly such that the firms, even when there are only two of them, compete to the extent of driving price up to the competitive level.
5. This corresponds directly to the notion of the Lerner index measuring monopoly power as the reciprocal of (the modulus of) the elasticity of demand, η such that the price-cost margin is $(p - MC)/p = 1/\eta$, which obviously increases as demand becomes more inelastic (essentially, the demand curve becomes steeper at the prevailing price). In the case of Cournot oligopoly, with constant returns to scale, this index is modified such that the weighted average price-cost margin is $(p - \Sigma_i MC_i s_i = H_Q/\eta$, where s_i represents the share held by firm i (i.e. $s_i = q_i/Q$) and H_Q is the Herfindahl concentration measure (i.e. the squared sum of market shares), and thus as concentration rises the weighted average price-cost margin rises (Clarke and Davies, 1982). With monopsony we find an equivalent expression, which Blair and Harrison (1993, p. 48) refer to as the Buyer Power Index (*BPI*), which measures the percentage deviation from the competitive result. Here, $BPI = (VMP_X - w)/w = 1/\varepsilon$, where VMP_X is the value of the marginal product, w is the factor price and ε is the elasticity of supply, measuring the responsiveness of the quantity supplied to a change in its price. The lower the value of ε, the greater is the

deviation from the competitive price. In the case of Cournot oligopsony, an equivalent expression can be derived in terms of the weighted average VMP to input price margin, such that $(\Sigma_i VMP_i \sigma_i - w)/w = H_X/\varepsilon$, where $\sigma_i = x_i/X$ is the share of total purchases made by firm i, implying that higher buyer concentration H_X, is positively related to greater departures from the competitive outcome – see Dobson (1990, pp. 50–3). In the case of a dominant buyer framework, Blair and Harrison (1993, p. 51) derive the buyer power index $BPI = S/[\varepsilon + \eta_f(1 - S)]$, where η_f is the elasticity of demand facing the fringe (assumed to be greater than that facing the dominant buyer) and S is their market share, such that the index is increasing in S and decreasing in ε and η_f.

6. As with collusion among sellers, there may be structural conditions which facilitate or, alternatively, impede collusion among buyers. For example, Blair and Harrison (1993) identify several factors which may facilitate collusion: (i) fewness of buyers (which keeps decision-making costs for the group down and enhances the ability to police agreements), (ii) product homogeneity (which simplifies the agreement to control of one price rather than a complex price schedule), and (iii) inelasticity of supply (since purchases only have to be reduced by a small amount to achieve a significant price reduction and the rewards from collusion are greater).

7. Here some qualification needs to be made particularly regarding joint purchasing behaviour since there may be obvious transaction cost savings associated with pooling resources to search and then negotiate contracts, giving rise to efficiency benefits from coordinated buying behaviour. Moreover, as Mathewson and Winter (1996) show, in the context of a monopolistically competitive selling market, a buyer group can gain by offering exclusivity contracts to a sub-set of potential sellers in exchange for a lower price with the result that welfare may increase. Here the parties to the agreement are better off but those consumers and firms outside of the agreement may be worse off. However, total welfare may increase as the buyer group may be a means of (partially) off-setting the tendency for a monopolistically competitive market to yield an inefficient trade-off between product variety or availability and lower prices. Specifically, where a market may yield too many suppliers (from a social welfare perspective), buyer groups can be a means of reducing the number of viable suppliers. For an alternative analysis and similar application to managed competition in health care markets, see Che and Gale (1997).

8. With flat supply curves, the buyers have nothing to exploit as price is the same for whatever level of purchases they decide upon. When the supplying industry is characterized by increasing returns it obviously has natural tendencies towards being a monopoly, or at least an oligopoly structure, in which case it is less likely that buyers will be in a position of (unilaterally) setting prices, and it is rather more likely that prices will be determined through negotiation. This case, with market power on both sides of the market, is considered in the next section.

9. For example, this latter point was made by the U.S. Supreme Court in its ruling on Northwest Wholesale Stationers Inc. v. Pacific Stationery and Printing Co., 472 U.S. 84 (1985). Here, Northwest Wholesale Stationers was a purchasing co-operative comprised of about a hundred office supply retailers and was viewed as allowing its members to enjoy the economies of large-scale purchases.

10. Here we are assuming that the monopsonist prices in its output market at a level equal to average cost ($p = AC_Q$), implying that it earns zero profits from the selling side of its operation.

11. A now standard approach to resolving this problem, following Rubinstein (1982), is to assume that the bargaining process is one in which parties make alternating offers/counter-offers and both are impatient to settle. Then, with complete information regarding each other's preferences, etc., and constant discount rates, the parties will (immediately) agree on a division of joint profits which yields them a share of the surplus generated according to their relative eagerness to settle.

12. Whether x_S is less than or greater than x_B clearly depends on the slopes and positions of the two sets of curves.

3. Buyer Power Propositions

Following on from our analysis of models of the effects of buyer power and following the standard welfare economic practice in Chapter 2 of considering social welfare without regard to distribution, we develop the following propositions:

- It is not the case that buyer power, by itself, is desirable. In fact, it is undesirable. To be specific, label a buying firm with buyer power as 'B', and firms from which it buys as 'Si'. Assume that the Si are in an essentially competitive industry, also that B has no selling power. An example might be a buyer who purchases potatoes from growers in a particular region of England, to sell on via wholesale markets. The analysis shows that social welfare, measured without regard to distribution, is lower than in the situation where the middlemen (firms like B) are numerous, all other things equal. Prices to growers are below those that would exist in a competitive market, but this causes output to be cut back and does not result in final consumers paying lower prices.
- Furthermore, if the firm with buyer power, B, has selling power as well, the situation so far as social welfare is concerned is worsened by comparison with the position above. To adapt the example, assume that potatoes from all regions of England are purchased by B and that because of their weight, the market for potatoes for sale in England largely consists of home-grown potatoes. Figure 2.2 shows the additional welfare loss created in this case.

Because these results, particularly the first, go against common beliefs, it is important to qualify them.

- It is relatively uncommon for there to be a single buyer, more common in food retailing is for there to be a limited number of buyers. We may assert that the direction of the effects identified above will be maintained, although they are likely to be smaller in magnitude. One particular circumstance is where a form of 'bidding war' between buyers, Bi, develops, such that they offer better and better deals to suppliers. The likely limiting result in this case is that prices paid to

21

growers approach the level they would expect in the absence of buyer power.

- There may be organisational economies in having a single buyer or a small group of buyers. For whatever reason, perhaps the transport technology, the timing and quantification of demand, or the availability of information about consumer preferences, there may be static and/or dynamic benefits in the supply chain taken as a whole from having dominant buyers. To extend the example, the buyer may notice in the market that potatoes coming from abroad differ somewhat in their characteristics, and that particular types are favoured by consumers. It is then feasible that the buyer suggests production strategies to the growers which will enhance their income.

It is where the selling stage, S, has an element of monopoly power that 'second best' results come into play and buyer power becomes more important. Let us first take the case where the buyer, B, does not have monopoly power downstream.

- Subject to caveats, where there is upstream seller power, the presence of a powerful buyer is likely to improve the position over what it would be if the buyer has no power. This happens for the following reason: left to their own independent devices, a powerful buyer and a powerful seller are likely to negotiate an outcome which improves both their positions. There is an obvious point of agreement on quantity, and the level at which the bargain on price settles, although important to the two parties, does not have an impact on overall social welfare. Assuming they reach this agreement, the quantity they transfer will be greater than the quantity either would envisage selling/ buying were the other party to have no market power. Thus the position with a powerful buyer is better than the situation with a powerful seller, S, alone.

- Even when S has monopoly power, this does not mean that social welfare is greater with the presence of a powerful buyer B who also has monopoly power in its own sales to customers than it is where S's monopoly power is the only distortion in the system. In fact, in simple cases these two scenarios (B as a monemporist, S as a monopolist, or S as a monopolist alone) are equivalent from a social welfare viewpoint. Again, the idea that buyer power is necessarily good must be qualified.

- However, B's buyer power is definitely desirable when B has no monopoly selling power and S has selling power. Here again, each of the players individually has a view about quantity exchanged and price for that exchange which are mutually incompatible, but we may expect them to recognise their mutual benefit in bargaining to a solution. This solution is also socially more desirable than either of the individual positions.

- There is an important further implication from this point. If it is inevitable that many suppliers of goods (say, powerful manufacturers) have some monopoly power, then it is also desirable that there exist buying groups which, while having no particularly powerful position in their final market, nevertheless have significant monopsony power.

- We may expect that in reaching bargaining solutions, given the range of uncertainties and other factors existing in practice, there will likely be significant non-linearities in pricing and other constraints in contracts. Thus, such aspects of contracts between the S and B levels should not necessarily be treated with suspicion, but rather on their merits and on the relative degree of concessions and constraints on each side.

- However, if one party makes all the concessions and the other accepts significant constraints, this would appear less like a genuine bargaining outcome and more like an imposition to enhance monopoly. For example, exclusivity agreed to by only one party may be an arrangement to enhance monopoly power through removing the possibility for substitution.

- All the above remarks relate to general tendencies given a set of underlying assumptions. It is clear that relative magnitudes of various effects will be influenced by such factors as relative degrees of market power, relative elasticities of the underlying curves, etc.

These propositions lead to the following suggested approach to investigating buyer power for policy purposes which draws upon Dobson, Waterson and Chu (1998).[1] The approach, set out in Table 3.1, is framed around five key questions dealing firstly with signs of market power at (i) the buyer level, (ii) the supplier level and (iii) the downstream level where the buyers sell on the goods/services, followed by consideration of the underlying economic conditions of production/distribution, specifically the nature of costs in the buying process, and lastly consideration of market behaviour with regard to the nature of trading relationships and potential anti-competitive practices.

The first question relates to the existence of buyer power. Unless one or more buyers have the ability materially to influence prices set or negotiated, or quantities exchanged, or impact on the viability of suppliers or competing buyers (so that it may be the case that the buyer acts against the public interest) then buyer power may be presumed to have no (notable) adverse welfare consequences.

However, given the presence of significant buyer power, the second and third questions respectively involve determining the extent of seller power at the supplier level (i.e. facing the buyers) and the extent of the selling power of the

Table 3.1 A framework for the analysis of buyer power

Question/Source	Relevant Evidence
1. Is there significant buyer power? This is essentially a qualifying question: if not, the considerations above are not relevant. By 'significant power' we mean the ability to have a material effect on prices set or negotiated, quantities exchanged, the viability of traders at one or more stages of production, etc.	• Significant proportions of the product as a whole purchased by a firm or group of firms. • Significant arrangement of terms of purchase by this firm or group of firms, such as upfront fees, slotting allowances, etc.
2. Is buying power against relatively powerless suppliers? If so, further investigation may be warranted. Alternatively, if there is also significant upstream seller power, there is less likely to be a problem.	• Absence of evidence that suppliers dictate terms of sale. • Low seller concentration in the upstream market.
3. Does the buyer itself have significant selling power? If so, then buyer power may serve as a means of strategically enhancing seller power in the downstream market with potentially adverse effects. On the other hand, if the buyer has no appreciable seller power, and the final market is generally competitive, its buying power is more likely to be socially desirable.	• Measures of assessing seller power in the downstream market. Here it will be important to investigate inter-relationships between the various actors involved.
4. Are there significant efficiency gains associated with buyer power? If so, then there may be an efficiency justification for buyers having market power.	• Pecuniary or organisational economies of scale or scope indicating a natural tendency for there to be few buyers, since average transactions costs are thereby reduced.
5. Does the buyer attempt to constrain its suppliers' other actions or deliberately create a dependency relationship? If so, such an arrangement should be treated with suspicion.	• Evidence of exclusive supply requirements, specific custom designs, idiosyncratic specification, etc. • Charging structures not obviously related to the cost structure of the goods specified.

Source: adapted from Dobson, Waterson and Chu (1998).

buyers (i.e. at the downstream level). In regard to the first aspect, if the buyer power is against relatively powerless suppliers then there are concerns about abuse of monopsony power, which might include a detrimental effect on producer (suppliers') surplus and the long term viability of suppliers. On the other hand, if buyer power is linked with significant seller power at the upstream level then it is more likely, *ceteris paribus*, that the existence or enhancement of buyer power is beneficial, that is buyer power may have a socially beneficial countervailing effect by negating the detrimental effects of upstream seller power. However, the overall effect on welfare in these circumstances will turn on whether or not the buyers themselves have significant selling power.

If it is the case that the buyers operate in a competitive output market as sellers, then buyer power is likely to have a benign countervailing impact on upstream selling power. In contrast, if buyer power is linked to (downstream) selling power then there are concerns that while buyer power may allow for a more (allocatively) efficient transfer of goods at the upstream stage there will be a detriment to welfare at the downstream level as the firms exploit their selling power. Judgement on the overall impact rests on which of the two effects is the stronger, i.e. the successive power arising from selling power at successive stages or the countervailing power effect arising from the presence of opposing (bilateral) market power. If final prices rise as buyers increase their bargaining power then the presumption is that the former effect dominates, *ceteris paribus*.

The fourth question is of particular relevance in assessing the impact of a merger between key buyers or co-operative buyer behaviour (i.e. the formation of a buyer group). Specifically, pooling resources to make purchases may yield efficiency benefits from reduced costs and consideration needs to be given to how great such benefits are when set against any anti-competitive effects. For example, there may be circumstances where the most productively efficient (i.e. least-cost) market structure on the buying side is a monopsony. In addition, pooling resources to make purchases such as through the formation of a buyer group may allow for reduced administrative and distribution/warehousing costs. However, for there to be a clear welfare benefit it should be the case that this collective purchaser power does not transfer through to increased selling power downstream, so that the benefits of any reduced costs are passed on to consumers.

Given the structure of power relations in the market addressed by the first three questions in Table 3.1, and efficiency effects associated with buyer power considered by the fourth question, the final question is specifically related to consideration of (potential) dependency relationships created by buyers (i.e. beyond simple quantity exchange at a fixed or negotiated price per unit). These actions are effectively vertical restraints induced by the buyer. Here the anti-competitive effects, which may serve to raise barriers to entry or mobility or serve to relax competition between existing rivals, need to weighed against potential efficiency benefits to determine the overall welfare effect.

It is envisaged that such a structured approach will prove particularly useful when undertaking case analysis, allowing for consistency in the analysis and effective comparisons to be made.

NOTE

1. This approach takes the same format of a table containing a series of questions and relevant evidence to answer them. However, it refines that approach to some extent in the context of a European perspective on this issue. In particular, we note that dependency relationships may cause specific concerns, where buyers may be regarded as exploiting their market power in a unfair manner.

4. Definition and Measures of Buyer Power

In order to operationalise the buyer power framework outlined in Chapter 3, it is important to be clear as to what is meant by the term buyer power and how it can be measured, in particular to respond to question one in Table 3.1. In this regard, this chapter considers the definition and various means of measuring buying power as well as commenting on the question of market definition as it relates to a purchasing market. Concerning measurement, we look at three potential classes of measure: buyer concentration, elasticities of supply and performance measures (such as price-cost margins). While all of these measures are potentially useful, from a practical point of view buyer concentration is likely to be most useful (a) because data on it are more readily available and (b) because there are difficulties of interpretation (and/or difficulties in collecting data) for the other possible measures. With these points in mind, we argue that buyer concentration measures, while they should not be used in isolation, are useful first indicators of possible buyer power problems.

4.1 DEFINITION OF BUYER POWER

It is useful to start with a general definition of buyer power. In their report on buyer power in 1981, the Committee of Experts on Restrictive Business Practices defined buyer power as 'a situation which exists when a firm or a group of firms, either because it has a dominant position as a purchaser of a product or service or because it has strategic or leverage advantages as a result of its size or other characteristics, is able to obtain from a supplier more favourable terms than those available to other buyers' (OECD, 1981).

More recently the Secretariat of OECD have offered an alternative definition which reflects differences in underlying negotiating power among contracting parties and is outcome-driven:

> ..a retailer is defined to have buyer power if, in relation to at least one supplier, it can credibly threaten to impose a long term opportunity cost (i.e. harmful or withheld benefit) which, were the threat carried out, would be significantly disproportionate to any resulting long term opportunity cost to itself. By disproportionate, we intend a

difference in relative rather than absolute opportunity cost, e.g. Retailer A has buyer power over Supplier B if a decision to de-list B's product could cause A's profit to decline by 0.1 per cent and B's to decline by ten per cent. (OECD, 1998, para. 20)

Common to both definitions is the view that firms will have market power as buyers, typically, when they have a dominant position in the market and they use this to extract favourable prices and other terms and conditions from suppliers.

However, this is not the only feature of buyer power that one might want to stress. From a policy point of view, buyer power is likely to be more of a problem where it results in discounts and additional favourable conditions which are not linked closely to savings in costs. If this is the case, price discounts will be discriminatory and larger, more powerful buyers (or buyer groups) will benefit at the expense of smaller firms. This, of course, was an important issue in the US in the 1930s, leading eventually to the 1936 Robinson-Patman Act which (controversially) outlawed such discriminatory behaviour (see Scherer and Ross, 1990, pp. 508–16).

In addition, buying power is also likely to be important, from a policy viewpoint, where firms have monopsonistic (or oligopsonistic) power. This will arise typically where there are broadly competitive conditions on the supply side of the market, and the supply curve is not perfectly elastic. If this is the case, the monopsonist (or oligopsonists) can exert their buying power by restricting demand and, thereby, purchase at less than the competitive price. Again, therefore, one might want to capture this aspect of the market in some measure of buyer market power.

4.2 MEASURES OF BUYER MARKET POWER

In measuring this concept, different families of measure focus on various specific aspects. The 'ability to have a material effect on prices' (Table 3.1) and more generally, the social impact of buyer power, relates both to the relative size and strength of buyers and the scope for exercising that strength. In principle, both matters are relevant to buyer power. The first set of measures discussed below refers to relative size, the second set to scope. The third set of measures focuses on outcomes rather than potential.

4.2.1 Buyer Concentration

The most straightforward summary measure of buyer power is buyer concentration. As the definition in the last section makes clear, buyer power is most likely to arise where one or a few firms (or buyer groups) dominate the buying side of the market. Therefore, we expect buyer concentration to be a useful first indicator of possible buyer power. As noted above, however, the existence of high buyer concentration need not imply that significant buyer power is being exercised (although, in many cases, it probably will) and hence other factors need also to be considered (e.g. the structure of the selling side of the market) before any strong conclusions can be drawn. Generally, buyer concentration can be said to relate both to numbers of buyers (negatively) and to size inequalities between them (positively).

There are various possible measures of buyer concentration, all of which are directly analogous to measures on the supply side of the market. One possible measure is the number of buyers who account for (say) 50 per cent of the purchases of a good. This measure is attractive because it is easy to calculate and has clear intuitive appeal. While, as with other concentration measures, the choice (in this case, of the percentage of output used) is largely arbitrary, the 50 per cent measure also has intuitive appeal. If, as is the case for some products, the leading five firms, say, purchase 50 per cent of some good, one might infer that buyer concentration is high. On the other hand, if, say, ten or more firms control 50 per cent of the market, then there is less evidence, all other things equal, that buyer power exists.

It is important, however, to qualify this in one way, in that, within the top ten firms, say, one (or several) firms may dominate the market (e.g. the leading firm may have 40 per cent of the market by itself). Hence, it is desirable to pay attention to the leading firms' market shares as well as this (or other) measures. Thus size inequalities are important, although it is relevant to note that there is no obvious or unique way in which to combine the two elements – particular concentration measures involve doing this in various ways.

One obvious summary measure (which we use in this study) is the buyer concentration ratio. In this case, as is well known, the focus is on the market share of the largest r firms buying in the market. If $r = 5$, then we measure the market share of the leading five firms. This measure is also easy to calculate and has strong intuitive appeal. For example, if the top five firms have shares of 20 per cent, 18 per cent, seven per cent, four per cent and three per cent, then the five firm buyer concentration ratio (BCR5) is 52.

Other measures of buyer concentration are also available (e.g. the Herfindahl index, the entropy index, and so on).[1] The Herfindahl index is widely used in measuring seller concentration, and could also be used here. In this case, the index measures the sum of the squared market shares of firms purchasing a particular product. While this measure has some advantages over traditional concentration measures (e.g. it takes account of all firms in the market), it has the disadvantage that it is more difficult to calculate since (estimates of) all market shares must be included to calculate it accurately, and it has less intuitive appeal. In fact, the Herfindahl index may be viewed as a special case of a more general weighting scheme defining a class of indices, each of which satisfies a set of criteria which are desirable for concentration indices to possess, as explained by Hannah and Kay (1977). For these reasons, we make use of the simpler concentration ratio (combined with data on leading firm market shares) in this study. It is a measure which we suggest can always be used in a first pass examination of a market's buyer power.

4.2.2 Elasticities of Supply

Blair and Harrison (1992) argue that buyer power can alternatively be measured by what they call the Buying Power Index (BPI), based on elasticity of supply. The argument is as follows. If we take the case of a monopsonist buyer of a good, then, in equilibrium, the extent of buyer power (measured as the difference between the amount the monopsonist is willing to pay for a good at the margin and the price that it does pay) is equal to the reciprocal of the elasticity of supply. Hence, one can measure the extent of buyer power by looking at (the reciprocal of) the elasticity of supply. This is a similar argument to that used by advocates of the Lerner index on the selling side of the market (Lerner, 1934). It examines the scope for buyer(s) to have an effect on the market, rather than their size.

The intuition underlying the point is that if a good is in perfectly elastic supply, even a monopsonist (with BCR=1) cannot exert buying power, despite being the dominant buyer in the market, through restriction of supply. However, if supply is less than perfectly elastic, the monopsonist can restrict demand and lower its buying price, and hence make monopsonistic returns. The less elastic is supply, the greater is a monopsonist's buying power. The authors also show (as noted in Chapter 2) that if there is a dominant buyer together with a competitive fringe, a similar argument can be made, although in this case the buyer power index depends also on the market share of the dominant firm and the elasticity of demand of the competitive fringe.

This approach is interesting in that it looks explicitly at the source of monopsony power. Supply inelasticity may be seen to be an important element in determining the overall impact of buyer power. However, it also has problems. As noted by Jacobson and Dorman (1992; see also Jacobson and Dorman, 1991) elasticities of supply are difficult to measure in practice, and hence, while it may in principle be suitable, this measure is less likely to be practical than the BCR. Added to this, the measure is only suitable within monopsony-type models; specifically, where there is perfect competition on the supply side of the market. In markets where this does not apply (e.g. with monopoly or oligopoly supply), the model is more complicated and this can be a practical limitation. Nevertheless, some markets relevant to the industry in hand are essentially competitive (in supply), for example the market for fresh produce. Therefore, particularly when BCR is very high, and despite the practical difficulties, it is likely to be worthwhile to attempt a calculation of this measure, or at least to survey the literature for estimates. This will enable some prioritisation of cases.

4.2.3 Performance Measures

A third approach is to measure buyer power by output or performance measures such as profitability or the price-cost margin. An obvious measure of buyer power in a monopsony-type model is the margin between the price the monopsonist is willing to pay (at the margin) and the price he does pay; or simpler still, the size of the discount to the competitive price. And, more generally, a direct measure of buyer power would be the size of the discount gained by the buyer (or buying group) and/or the value of any special terms it obtains from suppliers (net of any cost savings made in selling to a larger group). However such information is difficult to obtain, or, at least, would require considerable effort and expense to gather. Therefore the measure is not well suited to a preliminary investigation established to examine the a priori possibility of further investigation being required.

Less demanding would be details of the price-cost margins of the buying firms. However, price-cost margins reflect a number of different things and are not indicators of buying power alone. The problem of the foregone alternative is particularly severe here. Supermarket multiples may for example exert buying power in order to lower prices and increase price-cost margins, but price reductions might simply reflect reduced costs e.g. in handling or in buying in bulk rather than reflecting (additional) buying power. In this sense, high margins may not be undesirable in the eyes of society generally since the benefits could not be obtained in a market with competitive supply. Alternatively, supermarket multiples might exert buying power and achieve lower prices but also exert power at the retail stage, enabling them to increase their margins by more than implied by buyer power alone. Or high price-cost margins could be achieved by lowering costs at all stages of operation of the firm, rather than them arising from the buying power of the firm.

Two problems are evident in these examples. One is that price-cost margins of downstream firms depend on all stages of their operations and not just on buyer power in the upstream market. Second, price-cost margins themselves reflect two factors, prices and costs, and, at least on an a priori basis, one should not leap to the conclusion that they imply buyer (or seller) market power. Having said this, high price-cost margins could be indicative of such power. They should not in any sense be seen as determining the existence of potential problems, but they may be a useful indicator of cases to investigate further.

4.2.4 Practical Procedures

The discussion above suggests the following procedures might be considered by policy-makers dealing with the first question of Table 3.1. Within the relevant market, a measure of buyer concentration such as BCR5 should be prepared, price-cost margins calculated, and the literature surveyed for appropriate measures of supply elasticity, where feasible and relevant. Where BCR5 is high, where there is significant inelasticity in supply, and margins are high, the indication is that buyer power is of some importance, so that question one may be answered affirmatively. Of course, the approach should not be used slavishly and if individual market shares are available, they provide substantial additional information compared with BCR – they enable a distinction between a tight oligopoly and a dominant firm situation, for example. High margins, by themselves, are not a key feature in determining the need for further examination, but high BCR may be. The investigation will also have a bearing on question 2.

4.3 MARKET DEFINITION

Clearly, the definition of the market – whether it is broad or narrow – is an important issue in the assessment of market power. There are two key dimensions which require consideration here: the geographic extent of the market and the substitutability between products providing similar services. Potentially there are considerable differences between the appropriate definitions on the selling and the buying sides. For many goods, competition on the selling side may for practical purposes be limited, with consumers facing a limited number of stores within easy travelling distance in a given geographic area (so the relevant market is sub-regional) and with segmentation by retail service. In contrast on the buying side, the geographic market could be national or international, but because of the specific nature of supply for particular brands or items, the product dimension might turn out to be quite narrow. Moreover, individual suppliers may be economically dependent on particular distributors (especially where long-term supply contracts are a common market feature).

As a background, and general guide, we may take the European Commission's Notice on Market Definition (1997). Market definition on the sellers' side concerning the extent of the market depends on the question 'whether [given a particular definition] the parties' customers would switch to readily available substitutes or to suppliers located elsewhere in response to a hypothetical small permanent relative price increase to the products and areas being considered' (European Commission, 1997b) in such numbers as to make the price increase unprofitable. If so, the market definition must be broadened. This broadening (by product and/or area) continues until the question can be answered in the negative.

To take an example within which to consider the geographical extent of the market, we may consider electrical goods retailing. The market would be a sub-region if when all the electrical retailers in that area raise their prices by 5–10 per cent, insufficient customers search elsewhere (choose alternative shopping venues) to make the increase unprofitable. But if large numbers did buy elsewhere, the market would have to be broadened to, say, a region, or even a country.

However, the matter also depends on practice and time-scale. To take the more directly relevant example of UK supermarkets, if it is common practice for nationwide pricing to be adopted by most chains then consumers in fact do not have the opportunity to purchase elsewhere at different prices and the observation that prices and other aspects of format are aligned across a country indicates that the retailers do not believe separate markets are easily or fruitfully identified. Sometimes, data may be brought fairly directly to bear – the case of car price differentials between the UK and Continental Europe comes to mind. In this case, the market is clearly at most the UK (more probably a part of it), since various factors mean only small numbers of British customers search on the Continent despite what appear to be significant price differences. In the case of food retailing, we take the pragmatic view that the countries of the EU are significantly different from one another in terms of shopping habits that the most appropriate definition of the retail market is national as opposed to international. This is a relatively broad conception of the market and for some purposes, or in some countries, it would be thought too broad – one can imagine a gap in the chain of substitutes between areas of France, for example. However in practice, data at a finer level of disaggregation than national are not at all easy to obtain, so that a pragmatic definition would need to be at national level, geographically speaking. Of course this may mean that for some purposes, the true market concentration is understated by the data.

There is also the question of the product side of the definition. Again the test is whether customers would switch to substitutes in sufficient numbers if price rose 5–10 per cent over a sustained period. The operational issues in the particular case we examine here are whether to include discount stores and whether to include convenience stores. Given the developments in the relationship between discount stores and existing supermarket chains in some countries (e.g. Germany) and given the presence in some other countries (e.g. the UK) of a clear recognition of the importance of low price ranges to a significant group of consumers, we take the view that discount stores should be included in the definition. Their essential appeal is low prices and significant numbers of consumers seem willing to trade-off price against range. On the other hand, convenience stores satisfy a rather different and not very price sensitive market for 'top-up' products as opposed to a weekly shop. Hence we would aim not to include them in our definition of the market.

There is an important caveat to the Commission's test. The price concerned need not be the market price '...where the prevailing price has been determined in the absence of sufficient competition' (para 19). This caveat is important to avoid a logical contradiction, often known as the 'cellophane fallacy'. By definition a profit maximizing monopolist does not produce on the inelastic portion of a demand curve. Thus, from a monopoly price, it is not the case that increasing the price will be profitable. Yet a monopolist is the only firm in the market, so the market cannot be broader. Clearly, a less than monopoly price must constitute the appropriate benchmark from which to carry out the hypothetical test. Indeed, we would argue that the most appropriate price from which to carry out the test would be an essentially competitive price. Again, this may mean that a pragmatic approach to definition serves best.

Let us turn now to modifying the definition to tackle the question of market definition on the buyer's side. Consider the following proposal (of our own devising) which moves the question from purchasers to suppliers. The question is whether [given a particular product and geographical market definition] the parties' suppliers, faced by a 5–10 per cent permanent cut in the price they receive, would refuse to supply to the buyer(s) in such numbers that the price cut proposed would reduce the parties' range of goods sold to such an extent that the price cut was unprofitable.

This impact on profit would be likely to be felt because there would be insufficient throughput of goods of that type into the store(s) (in the case of the party being a retail buyer) in question, because there was then insufficient choice of goods for customers to be attracted to the store. Thus, of course, the definition ultimately relates to the end consumer, and the typical or general consumer's practices, since the demand by a buyer is derived from that of the final consumer. If the question was answered in the affirmative, the range of buyers (geographically or by type) would then be expanded to broaden the defined market until the answer is negative.

To take an example on the product side suppose an Italian clothing chain, specializing in designer clothing, seeks to impose a price cut on its suppliers coming from within a given geographical market: would sufficient of them refuse to supply that the chain then has very much less to offer the customer, so that significantly fewer people buy? Is the fall-off in sales sufficient to make the attempt to impose the price cut on suppliers unprofitable? If not, that chain constitutes a market on the buyers' side. But if so, the definition must be expanded to encompass more chains of a similar nature. If the answer was now 'yes', the market on the buyer's side would be defined. We can imagine that if all clothing stores of a particular type within a specified geographical area acted in the same way, producers would buckle under the stores' demands, but they may well be unlikely to do so when faced with a small chain acting unilaterally.

On the geographical side, the price cut described above might be imposed on local regional suppliers, national suppliers, or international suppliers. Again we could ask the question, given a set of products, at what geographical level would it be necessary to impose the hypothetical price cut in order to reduce the range significantly enough to render the cut unprofitable? For most products, including groceries, the impact of a price cut imposed by a 'hypothetical monopolist' upon suppliers from a particular region would be unlikely to have an impact.[2] The more likely levels of geographical market on the buyer side are national or international.

Again, custom and practice are of some importance. In the food producing industry (on the manufacturing side), major producers are often multinational. However negotiations are often carried out by retailers with national subsidiaries, and so the appropriate level at which to consider the geographic market in these cases is national. In other cases, however, negotiations take place at international level, and, in these cases, the EU level may be more appropriate.

On the product side, the market is certainly broader than food itself. A retailer which did not carry a range of household goods (detergents and other cleaning goods, paper products such as toilet tissue etc.) along with alcoholic as well as soft drinks, would be considered to have a poor 'offer' to consumers. The extent to which the definition needs to encompass fresh produce (fruit and vegetables, bread, uncooked meat etc.) may differ from country to country.

The 'cellophane fallacy' caveat discussed above is important also in this context: if the current buying price is already low, a further cut would not be feasible – a supplier may be prepared to liquidate rather than cut the supply price further. Hence, the impact of existing market power on the prevailing buying price must be recognised when engaging in the thought experiment – a competitive price is the best point from which to start the experiment.

To summarise on our definition of the food retail market for the purposes of this study, we take the market on both buyers' and sellers' side to be typically at the country level, geographically.[3] On the sellers' side, the product market includes conventional supermarkets/hypermarkets and discounters. On the buying side, the product market includes household goods and drinks in addition to foods as such.

4.4 ASSESSING THE IMPACT OF BUYER POWER IN SPECIFIC CASES

Against the definitional background of the previous parts of this chapter, and the propositions of the previous chapter, we next turn to some suggestions for evolving a methodology which might be employed to assess empirically the impact of buyer power in a particular case. It should be said at the outset, however, that the existing academic literature contains remarkably few empirical studies which have attempted to assess the impact of buyer power on prices, profits (or any other measures of firm behaviour or performance). In that sense, we tread more or less virgin territory.

Step 1: preliminaries   As always, the assessment should start with a rigorous definition of the appropriate market. This will be followed by a summary of the size distribution of the major players (in this case, of course, buyers) in that market.

Step 2: concentration   The potential for market dominance may then be deduced by estimating buyer concentration measures. There needs to be flexibility in identifying how many of the leading players to include in the concentration measure. In general, it is too simplistic to consider only the share of the largest firm, but, equally, summary statistics, such as the five firm concentration ratio, or Herfindahl or entropy indices will often gloss over important size differentials within the leading group. As is clear from Table 7.6 below, there are important differences between member states in the nature of the size distribution of firms within the top five: sometimes, the market can be characterised as a single dominant buyer, but more usually, a natural break suggests that the number of significant players will be between two and four. Similar remarks apply to measuring the concentration of food manufacturers.

Step 3: behaviour   Whatever the measure of structure, the potential for dominance is not the same as dominance itself. To go any further, it is necessary next to introduce information on behavioural and performance variables. As a general proposition, it is unlikely that behavioural indicators will provide conclusive evidence. Even assuming access to detailed information on buyer-seller contracts, how is it possible to deduce, without reasonable doubt, the relative bargaining strengths of the two parties in drawing up the contract? In general, therefore, we believe that outcomes are likely to provide the more conclusive evidence.

Step 4: analysis of performance outcomes   Given the well-known ambiguities of data on profitability (e.g. differing accounting conventions, disaggregating consolidated accounts, etc.), the assessment needs to focus inevitably on margins.[4] The retail/wholesale[5] mark up is the obvious starting point. However, it is necessary to control for factors which are product-specific, insofar as they influence the marginal cost of retailing the product (for example, frequency of purchase, perishability, volume-value ratios.) The word 'control' can only be defined rigorously once the scope of the empirical analysis has been set.

Hypothetically, consider the market for instant coffee. An analysis of whether there was 'high' buyer power in this particular market might be conducted econometrically using panel data across countries, time and products. The objective might be to assess whether retail mark-ups are especially high in this market (perhaps in a particular member state) relative to mark-ups earned elsewhere (in other product and/or geographic markets). If so, while the main focus of the analysis would be on the causal relationship running from structure to margins, it would be essential to include other explanatory variables reflecting the product characteristics just mentioned.

Assuming specificational issues such as these have received careful attention, the analysis of margins offers the best prospect for making an accurate assessment of the impact of buyer power. In principle, the aggregate mark-up of retail price over the sum of production and retail cost (M1) can be decomposed into the supplier's (manufacturer's) mark-up (M2) and the retailer's mark-up (M3).[6] Joint (systems) analysis of these three margins (and their changes over time) should provide evidence on whether buyer power has an impact which is at the expense of (i) the manufacturer only, (ii) the final consumer only, or (iii) both. A particular factor of relevance would be if the retail margin had been growing as the supplier margin was shrinking.

NOTES

1. See, for example, Clarke (1985).
2. Though for some products supply is local, e.g. locally grown vegetables.
3. Though we recognise that in some cases on the buyers' side, the market may be defined at the EU level, and in some cases on the sellers' side, it may take on a localised nature if nationally operating chains choose to adopt local pricing (which the flexibility of EPOS systems makes feasible) or competition is predominantly between regional and/or local operators.
4. The problem with price data (whether retail or wholesale) on their own is that trends may be influenced considerably by external factors such as the general economic environment which makes identifying causal mechanisms and associations with market power extremely difficult.
5. 'Wholesale' should be interpreted here as the factory gate price.
6. Practical problems involve allocating costs to specific products when these are shared with other products. For instance, the retail gross margin on product i (GM_i) may be straightforward to calculate as the retail selling price (p_i) less the unit purchase price (w_i) all divided by the retail price (i.e. $GM_i = (p_i - w_i)/p_i$). But the retail net margin for the good (NM_i) will also need to take account of the retail costs for selling the product (r_i), i.e. $NM_i = (p_i - w_i - r_i)/p_i$ where, with common display/shelving/store facilities, etc., the allocation of costs to a particular product line may, inevitably, be somewhat arbitrary. In addition, other (fixed) costs such as the price of land, taxes, etc. need also to be considered especially where cross-country comparisons are made.

5. Competition Policy and Buyer Power

The debate over the design of appropriate competition and anti-trust policy towards buyer power has developed considerably in recent times as the problem has taken on greater significance in light of the increased concentration of retail markets. Much of the literature has focused on US policy, and in particular criticisms of the Robinson-Patman Act – see Borghesani, de la Cruz and Berry (1997) for a thorough review of the relevant US policy and law. However, policy and law in the EU has also been the subject of recent debate – see for example Vogel (1998), Ratliff (1998) and for a comprehensive review, OECD (1998). This chapter briefly reviews the issues in the European context.

The European Commission's established position on buyer power is perhaps best set out in the Conference papers of the 'European Competition Forum, 1995' (see Ehlermann and Laudati, 1997). The discussion in this Forum suggests that various competition authorities should consider buyer power to be a real issue, something which is often exploited in an unacceptable manner, but not a practice which is easy to tackle under traditional notions of anti-trust and competition law. The issue is also viewed as more one for national than EC enforcement, given the marked disparity in market concentration and retail structures in different countries and the present reality that most buying activity is at most on a national scale (rather than on a cross-national or pan-European level).[1]

However, specific national legislation exists which is designed to combat the abuse of buying power based on 'economic dependency' notably in French[2] and German[3] law.[4] Thus, for instance, French law prohibits the abusive exploitation, by an undertaking or a group of undertakings, of the state of economic dependence of a customer or supplier who has no equivalent alternative. Such abuse can occur where there is a refusal to supply, tied sales, discriminatory conditions of sale or the breaking off of established business relations on the sole ground that the other party refuses to submit to unjustified conditions of business.

The kind of unacceptable practices considered range from the general extraction of non-cost justified rebates to listing fees, slotting allowances (shelf rental payments) and other charges which are forced on the supplier by the buyer after the original contract has been signed and agreed (i.e. mainly forms of post-contractual opportunistic behaviour).

In practice, the power of the retailer in buying comes from the sheer range and diversity of the products it stocks. Even a supplier that may have considerable market share (bringing it close to being classified as dominant on normal Article 82 principles) may not be in a position to resist a key retailer's demands. For the supplier, the retailer may represent a significant proportion of its overall sales, say 15 per cent, but for the retailer that 15 per cent may represent say only one per cent or two per cent of turnover, and thus the real power may lie with the purchaser and not the supplier. The purchaser wants the leading brands in its outlets but would not suffer that much, if it had to switch. It could also de-list the supplier's brands and put in its own brands. In some cases, it may be possible for the supplier to shift its supplies to other outlets in the event that it loses the customer, but often that is not true, which means that the supplier is, in practice, very much in the hands of the purchaser. Moreover, even losing one key retailer may mean that the supplier loses critical economies of scale, raising its average costs and placing it at a competitive disadvantage with other rival suppliers.

The various provisions in national law which exist focus on the idea that a party infringes competition law if it abuses a situation of economic dependence. However, what the discussion in the Forum showed is that these provisions had been hardly used since they were introduced. In large part this has been due to a reluctance on the part of suppliers to complain (for fear of reprisals). But even if a case is taken up it may well fail because of the requirements of showing (i) dependence, (ii) abuse and (iii) an effect on the market (which is notoriously difficult to show).

The overall conclusion is that the relevant provisions are not successful at present (though they may have some limited deterrent effect), and that abusive buyer power may be something that could be tackled better as a concept of unfair competition than as one of anti-trust. However, it should be evident that unfair competition is usually associated with property rights and in this context it would indicate that the issue is really over the division of economic surplus (profits) rather any detrimental impact on total economic welfare (which is the essence of concerns in competition policy).

Interestingly the French Ordonnance has since been strengthened in this direction by the Act of 1 July 1996.[5] This prohibits as involving the abuse of a situation of economic dependence:

- listing fee practices imposed by distributors on producers without any actual, proportionate quid pro quo (Article 36(3));
- the seeking of advantages under the threat of a sudden breaking-off of commercial relations (Article 36(4)); and
- the abusive breaking-off without notice of established commercial relations (Article 36(5)).[6]

The Competition Forum also discuss the use of EC competition law in these situations.[7] It is argued that it is possible to intervene on the basis of Article 81 if the buyer power in question is created through horizontal agreements. However, there may be problems showing an infringement. For example, the agreements are often not between competitors since the groups in question are established on different territories (i.e. not direct competitors when selling). Moreover, since the purchasing power of the group has to be weighed against concentration on the supply side, it may be viewed as falling outside Article 81 (1). In terms of using Article 82, the key issue is defining whether there is dominance on the part of the buyer. In this regard, the existence of 'entry' or 'listing fees' might be viewed as the compulsory remuneration of the supply listing service.

The extent to which 'economic dependency' as a concept is appropriate in the design of competition policy remains contentious. In so far as dependency may result in adverse welfare effects, say because short term gains (e.g. from retailer cost reductions) are outweighed by long-term detriment to efficiency (e.g. due to raised costs and/or reduced quality as a consequence of under-investment by suppliers) then it is of direct concern to competition policy. Otherwise, it may be better tackled under unfair competition laws – e.g. when it is simply a matter of distribution of economic rents. But apart from economic dependency there is still real concern that buyer power may distort both supplier and retailer competition, i.e. along standard horizontal market power concerns. In the United Kingdom, for example, the competition authorities have traditionally held the view that the power of the large supermarket chains has a positive effect since it brings down prices, and the benefit is generally passed on to the customer insofar as there is strong competition at the distributor level. This view is broadly supported in the recent Competition Commission (2000) investigation of this sector.

The overall conclusion is that, apart from standard horizontal concerns where buyer power goes hand-in-hand with seller power, these are issues which are not easily dealt with in EC competition law. There have been examples of wording applicable to buyer power and some cases,[8] but for the moment these are issues which are more likely to be dealt with at a national level at least where appropriate laws are in place.

Nevertheless, beyond the issue of buyer power *per se* and its impact on supplier viability and other problems arising through economic dependency relationships, EC competition law has special bearing on other aspects, notably vertical restraints. Of course, in practice, key manifestations of buyer power arise through retailers placing contractual obligations on suppliers which go beyond the simple specification of price and quantity to be transacted – for example, exclusive supply obligations, slotting allowances, listing fees, and retroactive discounts. Such buyer-induced vertical restraints, as with all other classes, can have both pro- and anti-competitive effects (see Dobson and Waterson, 1996, Dobson et al., 1998 and OECD, 1998 for a discussion).

The EC policy treatment of vertical restraints has recently been the subject of much debate and reappraisal, with the release of the EC Green Paper (European Commission, 1997a), and new proposals have subsequently been forthcoming (though a number of key revisions have yet to be finalised). New standard block exemption rules will apply across all sectors so that vertical restraints associated with retailers will receive the same treatment as restraints induced by producers. Buyer-induced restraints like exclusive supply obligations will generally be treated as being neither blanket-prohibited nor, at the other extreme, freely permitted, but instead subject to market share rules – such that below a critical threshold (yet to be determined, but possibly around the 30 per cent mark) a firm may receive an exemption in regard to Article 81 (1), but above this level the practice could be investigated and, if found to be against the public interest, then prohibited.

In addition, the new block exemptions rules have a particular bearing on retailer alliances – viewing them essentially in terms of a vertical arrangement rather than simply a co-operative horizontal one. The suggestion is that associations of independent retailers could be permitted to benefit from block exemption regulations, provided that the independent retailers are small and medium-sized enterprises, the market share of the association remains below a certain threshold (20 per cent) and that there are no territorial sales restrictions or other 'horizontal aspects' which violate Article 81 (like price-fixing).

This approach clearly has both an economic and social aspect in potentially benefiting smaller businesses by allowing them to compete more effectively with large, integrated retail groups. Moreover, this approach is somewhat similar to national law in some member states – notably Sweden, Denmark and Finland – which provide similar chain co-operation clearances. For instance, the so-called 'ICA' block exemption in Sweden (named after the major grocery chain of that name) provides a general exemption in Article 6 of the Swedish Competition Act for retail businesses which co-operate in chains, provided that their market share is not more than 20 per cent of the relevant market. Practices exempted are those involving restrictions in co-operation on purchasing, common marketing, common setting of prices in common marketing, assistance with calculations, the reservation of rights to sell goods commonly purchased, and co-operation on business establishment, financial and administrative tasks and business/personnel development.

In the case of Denmark, certain agreements regarding chain co-operation are excluded from the prohibition in Article 6 of the Danish Competition Act provided the chain has less than a 25 per cent market share and the arrangements do not infringe a defined 'black list' of practices. Among other things, participants in a chain co-operation can be obliged to buy the assortment which the chain co-operation commonly markets, to buy a minimum quantity of the commonly bought products and follow ordering, invoicing and payment procedures, to market the chain and commonly bought products according to agreed patterns, not to participate in or have economic involvement with other competing chain operations, and to obtain approval from the other participants on the location of new business premises. However, the exemption does not apply if the participating businesses are prevented from (i) buying and marketing other products or services than those in the chain co-operation agreement, (ii) marketing their own businesses, and (iii) lowering their prices directly or indirectly.

In Finland, general exemptions exist for a retail chain's price co-operation for national, regional and local special offer campaigns in the consumer goods field, provided that a certain market share is not exceeded. Thus, for instance, the Finnish Office of Free Competition issued a one year exemption for local campaigns by marketing rings in the Kesko K-Group, provided that the market shares of those concerned did not exceed 20 per cent.

Such exemptions in individual national member states, as well as the proposed change to EC law and policy, permit a greater coordination of business practices by formally independent businesses. This may permit members to benefit from scale and scope advantages and place them on a more equal competitive footing with large integrated retail groups, and thus promote a degree of retail diversity, particularly if it helps stem the decline of small independent businesses. Though, on the buying side, the effect will clearly be to raise buyer concentration which may exacerbate any economic dependency problems facing suppliers (particularly as the high threshold levels may permit such chains to have significant buyer power in their own right), yet it could conceivably benefit suppliers if it promotes more effective retail competition and provides an effective alternative means for producers reaching consumers (i.e. weakens the tight gate-keeper position of leading retailer groups).

NOTES

1. However cross-border alliances are growing; for a discussion see Chapter 7.
2. Article 8(2) of the 1986 Ordonnance.
3. Section 22 and 26(3) of the German Act on Restraints on Competition which came into effect on 1 January 1999.
4. Related laws also exist in Portugal, Spain and Greece.
5. Loi Galland. Similarly, Germany and Portugal have recently strengthened their provisions against abuse of economic dependency. Germany has introduced 'presumptions' of dependency in order to simplify proof of dependency and its competition law has been amended to include a prohibition of loss-leading. Portugal has added a series of *per se* prohibitions against 'abusive bargaining practices' which can be enforced within a complaint being filed.
6. See EC Commission Competition Report (1996), pp. 320–1; Lamy Droit Economique, 1998, p. 501.

7.   In particular, see pages 210–15.
8.   For instance, *Filtrona Tabacalera* (EC Commission Competition Report, 1989 at point 61).

PART II: STATISTICAL ANALYSIS

This part of the book includes most of the formal statistical analysis. It provides a bridge between the theoretical discussion of Part I, and the case studies of Part III. Thus, one purpose is to quantify some of the concepts just defined (e.g. buyer and seller concentration) for the EU retail food sector – both for individual member states and for the EU in aggregate. In addition, it sets the backcloth, or perspective, for the more in-depth case study analysis of three specific countries, and three specific products, described in the following chapters.

It includes two chapters. The first, Chapter 6, draws on existing statistical sources to build up a series of specially constructed tables. These are designed to provide a succinct summary of what is, in fact, a very disparate, often inconsistent, literature. In that sense, it is our interpretation of what is the 'received picture' of the key structural dimensions of the sector. Chapter 7 has a more ambitious objective. It constructs an entirely new database – the EU Retail Food Market Share Matrix – which is designed to yield an integrated, and internally consistent, statistical mapping of the structure of the sector at both the aggregate EU and national levels, and for the leading firms therein. We believe that this provides additional insights on some elements of structure, such as aggregate EU concentration and cross-border production, while improving the quality of information on others, e.g. measures of concentration at the national level. It also provides background information of relevance to our selection of case studies and analysis of merger activity and cross-border alliances.

6. An Overview of Market Structure Based on Existing Sources

This chapter is structured around 12 tables. Its objective is to draw on existing work to provide an opening picture of some of the salient features of market structure. In effect, it draws on existing studies and in that sense it is not original. However, the existing literature is extremely disparate and variable in the quality of its estimates. In providing our own overview, therefore, we have exercised considerable judgement in selecting and reporting only those estimates which we judge to be reliable and not internally inconsistent. We have also attempted to provide a synthesis which is wider in scope than any existing survey of which we are aware. Nevertheless, various gaps are apparent, and some elements of structure clearly require more systematic documentation. The next chapter will attempt to fill in some of those gaps.

6.1 MARKET SIZE AND THE SIZE OF RETAIL OUTLETS (Tables 6.1–6.3)

There is a rich academic literature within industrial organisation which explores the relation between size of market, the number of selling outlets and the size of those outlets.[1] This information can provide important insights into the nature of the underlying competitive process. In this particular context, there are two important dimensions.

- Over time, we know that there has been a continued decline in the number of retail food outlets in most, if not all, member states (e.g. Tordjman, 1994). This is apparently confirmed here by comparing columns 3 and 5 in Table 6.2. However, the two sources from which they are derived are clearly incompatible, and this provides a salutary example of how care must be taken in constructing internally consistent databases.[2] Across member states, there is obviously considerable variation. Table 6.1 reports the evidence at the aggregate level of all retailing, while Table 6.2 is confined to food retailing in particular.

47

Table 6.1 Size of the retail market as a whole across member states

	Per capita GNP ($000) 1995	Population 1995 (mn)	Number of retail outlets ('000)	Inhabitants per outlet	Retail sales (ecu bn)	Retail sales per outlet (ecu '000)
Germany	27.5	81.9	415.3	196	373	898
France	25.0	58.1	343.4	169	292	850
UK	18.7	58.6	289.9	202	233	803
Italy	19.0	57.3	627.2	91	311	496
Spain	13.6	39.3	440.2	89	89	202
Netherlands	24.0	15.4	123.3	125	61	494
Belgium/Lux	25.7	10.6	110.0	92	33	300
Greece	8.2	10.4	170.7	61	25	147
Portugal	9.7	9.9	130.4	76	26	200
Sweden	23.8	8.8	52.8	167	29	547
Austria	26.9	8.1	37.7	214	31	822
Denmark	29.9	5.2	40.9	128	28	684
Finland	20.6	5.1	31.7	162	22	694
Ireland	14.7	3.6	35.9	101	12	334
EU15 Total		372.3	3236.5	115	1565	549

Sources: For GNP and population, World Bank, 'World Atlas 1997'; for number of outlets and their sales, Corporate Intelligence on Retailing, as reported in 'The European Retail Handbook 1998' for the latest available year.

Table 6.2 Numbers of retail food outlets across member states

	Population 1995 (mm)	Number of food outlets 1996/7 ('000)*	Inhabitants per outlet 1996/7	Number of food outlets 1992/3 ('000)**	Inhabitants per outlet 1992/3
Germany	81.9	73.6	1111	44	1883
France	58.1	34.8	1667	87	670
UK	58.6	33.9	1667	60	975
Italy	57.3	114.6	500	296	193
Spain	39.3	79.0	476	177	223
Netherlands	15.4	6.0	2500	21	748
Belgium/Lux	10.6	13.0	769	37	289
Greece	10.4	17.2	588	54	194
Portugal	9.9	27.3	344	53	188
Sweden	8.8	6.2	1428	14	609
Austria	8.1	7.2	1111	7	1157
Denmark	5.2	3.2	1667	12	446
Finland	5.1	4.1	1250	7	743
Ireland	3.6	9.5	370	9	383
EU15 Total	372.3	429.4	867	876	425

Sources: * La Distribution Alimentaire; AC Nielsen, 1998; ** 'Retailing in the European Economic Area', EUROSTAT, 1996.

- In general (and as might be expected), the larger member states tend to have more retail outlets. However, the number does not rise proportionately with population size, and this means that, when judged by the number of inhabitants served by each outlet, Germany, the UK and France tend to have the highest rankings, and Portugal, Greece and Ireland the lowest.

Given that a larger inhabitant per outlet ratio will translate, *ceteris paribus*, into higher turnover per outlet, there are obvious implications for the differential ability of retailers from the different member states to achieve scale economies. Quite obviously, this suggests that full exploitation of scale economies in the smaller member states may only be possible for a limited number of firms, giving rise to the possibility that there will be natural oligopolies. Moreover, some members currently record an 'inhabitants per outlet' rating which is relatively low, given the size of the national market. This is especially true for Italy and (to a slightly lesser extent) Spain. (The reverse is true for Austria and, to a lesser extent, the Netherlands and Scandinavian countries). This is sometimes ascribed historically to cultural north-south factors, but, whatever the reason, there might be the a priori expectation that future consolidation of outlet size will be greatest in Italy and Spain.

Table 6.3 Comparison of the EU retail sector with Japan and the USA

	Population (mn)	Number of enterprises ('000)	Population per enterprise	Turnover (mn ecu)	Turnover per enterprise ('000 ecu)
EU15	372.3	2553	146	1261	494
USA	263.1	1530	171	1350	883
Japan	125.2	1519	82	682	449

Source: Derived using Panorama of EU Industry, 1997, Table 5, p. 21-15.

To add a wider perspective, Table 6.3 compares the EU as a whole with Japan and the USA. Judged on this evidence, the member states (EU15) have 'too many' retail outlets compared to the USA, given their comparative sizes. However, 'too many' is an ambiguous term, and this comparison probably only carries much meaning if one believes that the current level of integration within the states of the USA provides a useful indicator of what is to come with ongoing European integration. Japanese outlets, on the other hand, serve far fewer inhabitants than their European counterparts – as might be expected given the smaller population, although there is far less difference when judged by average turnover.

6.2 CONSUMER DEMAND (Table 6.4)

There are a number of reasons why the nature of the competitive process might be sensitive to the demand growth environment. These range from the obvious (e.g. the well-known empirical regularity that new entry is more common in growing markets) to the more theoretically subtle (e.g. the possibility that collusive outcomes are more/less likely in periods of recession/boom.)

Table 6.4 Growth in demand by member state

	% growth in total retail sales volume, 1990–94	Value of food sales 1996 (1990=100)
Austria	n.a.	113.4
Belgium/Luxembourg	6.9	130.7
Denmark	6.4	123.8
Finland	n.a.	95.2
France	5.8	113.4
Germany	6.5	111.4[b]
Greece	-10.8	147.2[c]
Ireland	12.0	130.1
Italy	1.0[a]	139.9
Netherlands	7.9	117.4
Portugal	n.a.	180.3
Spain	n.a.	132.5
Sweden	n.a.	109.1
UK	8.6	140.0

Note: [a] 1992–94; [b] base=1991; [c] value in 1994.

Sources: Total retail sales, corrected for inflation, are derived from data in Table 2, p. 21–14 of 'Panorama of EU Industry 1997', EUROSTAT; value of food sales are extracted from the individual country tables in 'The European Retail Handbook', 1998. These figures are for values, and are not corrected for differential inflation. The definition of 'food' varies considerably between countries. It invariably includes drink and tobacco, and often other products.

While it should be acknowledged that 'food' is an heterogeneous grouping which will include many specialist product lines of a 'luxury' (i.e. income-elastic) nature, there is little doubt that, in aggregate, it will have an income elasticity which is well below unity. What this means is that long-run demand is unlikely to exhibit dramatic growth (or cyclicality).

Given, moreover, the absence of much growth at all in the aggregate European macro-economy, the results shown in Table 6.4 are unsurprising.

- Retail sales in aggregate grew only very sluggishly in real terms during the first part of the 1990s (column 1 of Table 6.4). Among the member states shown, only Ireland achieved double figure growth between 1990 and 1994 (equivalent to an average annual growth rate of 2.9 per cent), and annual average rates of between 1.5 and two per cent were the norm.
- Reliable comparable estimates of real growth in retail food sales are elusive — the figures in column 2 of the table are uncorrected for price inflation — but, judged in nominal terms, it appears that the average annual growth rate, 1990—96, was only between two and five per cent in most cases. Allowing for inflation, this implies that real growth must have been extremely sluggish although this might also be attributable to falling real food prices in some countries.

Against this aggregate backcloth, it is clear that individual firms can only have achieved significant growth of turnover in real terms by increasing domestic market share, or from excursions into other member states, or by diversification beyond food retailing.

6.3 NATIONAL CONCENTRATION (Table 6.5)

In spite of the ready availability in the existing literature of market share and concentration estimates for most of the member states, it is by no means clear that previous calculations have been made on a like-for-like basis. Again, there is a variety of reasons why international comparisons are hazardous.[3] With this qualification, Table 6.5 presents the most recent available comparison across member states in CR5 – the five firm concentration ratio (showing the share of total food retail sales accounted for by the five largest firms), combined with estimates of how concentration has changed within each member state in recent years. The latter are probably the more reliable because similar accounting conventions are more likely to have been used when comparing a given country at two points in time than when comparing different countries at the same point in time. The table shows:

- Concentration has risen significantly in most member states in recent years. On the evidence of this table, this trend has been pervasive,

Table 6.5 Five firm concentration ratios for food retailing

	Current Level*	Change in recent years**		Source
		Per cent points	Period	
Austria	79	+14	1990–96	'Regal' 1997
Belgium/Luxembourg	57	+1	1988–92	AIM
Denmark	(78)	-	-	'Food Business'
Finland	96	+3	1990–96	Nielsen, Finland, 1997
France	67.2	+7	1988–92	AIM
Germany	75.2	+10	1988–92	AIM
Greece	(59)	-	-	The Retail Pocket Book 1998
Ireland	50	-	-	
Italy	30	-	-	
Netherlands	79	-	-	
Portugal	52	-	-	
Spain	38	+11	1988–92	AIM
Sweden	87	+24	1985–96	Supermarket Svenska Detaljhandel, 1997, for Food and Daily Goods
UK	67	+7	1988–92	AIM

Note: These estimates are drawn exclusively from previous studies. See Table 7.4 in Chapter 7 for our own estimates, based on the market share matrix.

Sources: * The current level is for the latest available year, as reported in 'La Distribution Alimentaire, 1998' (except for Denmark and Greece, for which the source is as shown in the final column). The sources for 'changes in recent years' are various, and as shown. They are not necessarily directly comparable with the current levels.

although it appears that the largest rises have tended to occur in member states in which concentration was, initially, more moderate.

To some extent, the latter finding is inevitable, given that CR5 is bounded from above. More substantively, however, it may reveal convergence across the member states.

- Whether or not there has been a tendency to convergence significant differences between member states still remain. Currently, concentration is highest in the small northern member states, and lowest in the southern states. Germany, the UK and France lie somewhere between the two extremes.

Two additional points are noteworthy. First, the estimate for Germany needs to be treated with extreme caution. Other contemporary estimates place German CR5 at much lower levels (the difference depending on whether buying groups are treated as single entities.) Second, and more substantively, the traditional expectation from Industrial Organisation was that concentration will tend to be lower, *ceteris paribus*, in larger markets (which are able to support more efficient-scaled firms). On this expectation, concentration should be lowest in Germany, France and the UK. The fact that this is not so suggests that this is a market in which sunk costs may be endogenous to the oligopoly game (whereby increases in market size encourage firms to escalate their sunk costs such as marketing, see Sutton, 1991). As such, the larger size of the market does not necessarily support more small-sized firms because they must be that much larger to compete with the market leaders.

This table, in particular, should be treated as provisional, pending the derivation of our own estimates in the next chapter, in which we are careful to distinguish buyer and seller concentration, and to employ consistent criteria of measurement.

6.4 THE CHANGING FACE OF RETAIL OUTLETS
   (Tables 6.6–6.9)

Both from casual empiricism and previous studies, it is clear that the face of food retailing has undergone a major shift in recent decades. Due to the spread first of supermarkets and then of hypermarkets, the demise of the traditional counter-service family-run store has been dramatic and probably irreversible.

- The diffusion of hypermarkets (columns 2 and 3 of Table 6.6) is obviously well under way, but incomplete, in all member states.

According to these figures, it is most advanced in the UK and France (in line with their relatively high concentration levels). In most other countries, there is relative uniformity, with the hypermarket market share lying in the region 10–20 per cent – with the exception of the two Iberian countries (both of which, interestingly, have seen a significant presence (and growth) of large French retailers.) In nearly all countries, however, the increase in their market share since 1980 has been significant.

- The rise of the supermarket, on the other hand, appears to have peaked, with, typically, less dramatic growth in their share during the 1990s.

Table 6.6 Grocery turnover by store type

	Hypermarkets		Supermarkets		Others
	1996	Change	1996	Change	1996
	%	since 1980	%	since 1990	%
Austria	12	+3	52	+11	36
Belgium/	16	-	70	+5	14
Luxembourg					
Denmark	17	n.a.	59	+8	24
Finland	22	n.a.	51	-1	27
France	51	+16	44	-	5
Germany	24	+8	52	+7	24
Greece	5	+5	51	n.a.	44
Ireland	12	n.a.	41	n.a.	47
Italy	13	+13	39	n.a.	48
Netherlands	5	+3	82	+7	13
Portugal	42	+42	28	+10	30
Spain	34	+22	25	+5	31
Sweden	13	n.a.	64	+4	23
UK	45	+29	42	+2	13

Note: These figures are for percentages of national aggregate turnover accounted for by each type of outlet.

Sources: AC Nielsen, *The Retail Pocket Book*, 1998; *La Distribution Alimentaire*, 1998.

Obviously, this is in part due to the rise of the hypermarket and in part to their already high share at the turn of the decade. Nevertheless, there remains considerable scope for growth in both forms in some member states – notably Italy, Ireland and Greece.

- The other major selling development has been in the rapid growth of discount stores.

As can be seen from Table 6.7, they increased their market share in all member states between 1991 and 1996 – typically by between five and seven percentage points, although strangely (in the light of the previous point) by ten per cent in Italy. This may suggest the emergence of a dual industry in that country, the reasons for which deserve further attention. In the next chapter, we identify the role of specific firms (for example, Aldi and Lidl) in this development.

Table 6.7 Growth in numbers of discount stores

	1996		1991		Growth in share
	No. of stores	% of national turnover	No. of stores	% of national turnover	(Per cent points)
Austria	568	17	530	14	3
Belgium/Lux	762	25	587	18	7
Denmark	739	20	544	15	5
Finland	820	12	760	10	2
France	1940	7	436	1	6
Germany	12130	30	8290	24	6
Greece	n.a.	n.a.	n.a.	n.a.	n.a.
Ireland	n.a.	n.a.	n.a.	n.a.	n.a.
Italy	2360	10	60	-	10
Netherlands	607	13	482	10	3
Portugal	314	9	30	2	7
Spain	2315	9	1180	5	4
Sweden	305	11	166	6	5
UK	1440	11	1129	6	5

Sources: AC Nielsen, The Retail Pocket Book, 1998.

In general terms, franchising is an organisational structure which can be used to gain a leading market position without necessarily incurring the same magnitude of sunk costs as would full-fledged ownership. Table 6.8 shows the number of franchisers and, in most countries, franchisees have increased in 1993–94. However, this table covers all retailing and hence should be treated with care.

With the growth of the hypermarket in particular, new opportunities for scale economies and innovation have emerged. Perhaps most significant of all is the growing use of electronic scanning at the check out.

Table 6.8 Franchising across the member states

	Number of franchisers		Number of franchisees	
	1993	1994	1993	1994
Austria	80	170	2500	2700
Belgium/Lux	90	135	3200	2495
Denmark	42	42	500	500
Finland	n.a.	n.a.	n.a.	n.a.
France	500	500	30000	30000
Germany	370	420	15500	18000
Greece	n.a.	n.a.	n.a.	n.a.
Ireland	20	n.a.	n.a.	n.a.
Italy	318	361	16100	17500
Netherlands	331	340	12640	12120
Portugal	55	70	n.a.	n.a.
Spain	117	250	14500	20000
Sweden	200	200	900	900
UK	373	396	18100	24900
EU Total	2496	2884	113940	129115

Source: Retailing in the European Economic Area, 1996, Table 14, p. 18, EUROSTAT.

Table 6.9 Diffusion of electronic scanning (number of EAN scanning stores) across member states (in hundreds)

	1994	1991	1987	1981
Austria	47	-	-	-
Belgium/Luxembourg	35	0.1	-	-
Denmark	27	0.1	-	-
Finland	32	-	-	-
France	200	66	16	-
Germany	149	73	10	0.2
Greece	-	-	-	-
Ireland	3	1	0.1	-
Italy	68	37	5	0.1
Netherlands	30	11	4	-
Portugal	44	3	-	-
Spain	115	50	2	-
Sweden	60	-	-	-
UK	180	60	8	0.1
EU Total	990	-	-	-

Source: Panorama of EU Industry, 1997, Table 11, p. 21-19.

- The diffusion of scanning has been rapid in recent years. In all (except one, again Italy) for which data are available, its usage at least doubled between 1991 and 1994 (Table 6.9). Assuming a further acceleration post-1994, it must, by now, have become a significant feature in the operations of many of Europe's leading retailers.

Not only does this technology permit a variety of internal economies, but also it provides the retailer with a rich source of detailed information about, for example, the elasticities of demand for specific brands. Undoubtedly, this has sharpened the retailer's capabilities – both in competing with its rivals and in bargaining with its suppliers, the food manufacturers.

6.5 INCREASED UPSTREAM CONTROL BY RETAILERS (Tables 6.10 – 6.12)

Of course, a number of the features already described have fairly obvious implications for the buying (as well as the selling) power of retailers, but this section considers four additional features.

- The retailers' 'private (own) labels' account for a significant and increasing proportion of total turnover.

The data reproduced in Table 6.10 are taken from different sources which, once more, are likely to be incompatible across a run of years. However, we have been able to locate two comparable pairs of years for most countries, together with an up-to-date picture for 1997 for the countries in which penetration seems most pronounced. This is sufficient to draw the following conclusions, which are best treated in an ordinal, as opposed to cardinal, manner. First, private label penetration is highest among a cluster of countries which includes the UK, France, Germany and the Benelux countries. Among these, it is most pronounced in the UK, least pronounced in Germany with the other three countries somewhere in between.[4] Evidence for the other member states is rather more patchy. However, such as it is, it suggests that private labels are less pronounced in the southern and the Nordic states. Second, all of the evidence shows increasing penetration (or, at least, no fall in penetration) in all countries over time. From the table, it is clear that this was particularly rapid during the 1980s for the four countries shown. Further advances were also made during the first half of the 1990s in the UK, Belgium, Germany and Spain, but not in France or the Netherlands. The most recent data, for 1997, are unfortunately not directly comparable with those for the earlier years. For this reason, one cannot say for certain whether the growth in private labels during the 1980s was sustained throughout the 1990s although our best guess might be that it was.

- Another crucial, and very particular, feature of the retailing industry, as opposed to most others, is the prevalence of 'buying groups'.

Table 6.10 Private label penetration by member state (%)

	1997	1995[a]	1992[a]	1990[b]	1980[b]	By leading retailers (1993/4)
UK	42.3	29	25	31	22	Sainsbury 55; Tesco 46; Argyll 38; Asda 32
Belgium/Lux	24.9	22	16	-	-	
Netherlands	19.1	16	16			
France	18.2	16	16	20	11	Monoprix 28; Casino 25; Intermarché 23; Carrefour 22; Auchan 19; Leclerc 10
Denmark	-	13	-	-	-	
Germany	12.6	11	6	24	15	Aldi 90; Metro 33; Tengelmann 18
Spain		10	8	9	2	Eroski 24; Pryca 20; Alcampo 15
Portugal	-	9	-	-	-	
Austria	-	9	-	-	-	
Finland	-	8	8	-	-	
Sweden	-	8	8	-	-	
Italy	-	6	4	-	-	
Greece	-	3	-	-	-	

Note: These estimates have been taken from a variety of sources. While the inter-country comparisons within each year (i.e. down each column) are comparable, only the years marked with identical [a] or [b] are comparable with each other. Thus, 1980[b] and 1990[b] are comparable (Nielsen/PLMA/Mintel from 'The Grocer' 8 May 1993); 1992[a] and 1995[a] are comparable (AC Nielsen, 'Private Label European Share and Price Trends, 1992–95'). The 1997 estimates are reported here as the most recent (AC Nielsen, reported in 'Food Business News', July 1998).

In some cases, these are consortia of (often small) independent retailers who combine for the purposes of enhancing their joint purchasing power. In other cases, the groups appear to be more closely linked through quasi-joint ownership. On a substantive level, the existence of these groups means that there is an important distinction to be made between seller concentration in the retail market and buyer concentration with respect to the manufacturers. On a statistical level, many of the existing data sources, unfortunately, treat these groups in different ways, sometimes combining the sales of constituent firms, but sometimes not. For this reason, we shall not report the results from previous studies here, leaving an assessment of their impact to the next chapter.

- Partly because of the strength of leading retailers and the existence of buying groups, independent wholesalers appear to have a relatively minor role in the food chain.

Table 6.11 The EU's top 20 grocery wholesalers

	Country of origin	Sales (bn ecus)
Nestlé	Switzerland	38.2
Food Ingredients Specialities	Switzerland	38.1
Rewe	Germany	14.6
Sandoz Nutrition	Switzerland	10.7
Casino Guichard Perrachon	France	9.5
Coop Valais	Switzerland	7.3
Spar Handels	Germany	6.9
Edeka	Germany	6.3
Faellesforenigen for Danmarks	Denmark	3.0
Booker Belmont	UK	2.9
SEITA	France	2.4
Nurdin & Peacock	UK	2.0
Merkur	Switzerland	2.0
Ramsvita	Switzerland	2.0
Tengelmann	Germany	1.8
Hofer & Curti	Switzerland	1.7
Systeme U Centre Regional Ouest	France	1.6
Schuitema	Netherlands	1.4
Skandinavisk Holding	Denmark	1.3
Fyffes	Ireland	1.1

Note: All figures relate to 1994, except Edeka (1993).

Source: *Panorama of EU Industry*, 1997, Table 6, p. 21-8.

As an illustration, Table 6.11 reproduces a list of the 20 largest European grocery wholesalers. The striking feature of this table is its heterogeneous nature. Note, for example, the leading role of the wholesaling activity of the French cigarette manufacturer SEITA, the leading position of Nestlé (a manufacturer), the relatively low ranking of UK wholesalers (in spite of the size

Table 6.12 The world's leading food and drink manufacturers in EU manufacturing

	World food sales ($US bn)	Total sales in EU food manufacture (bn ecus)	Markets in which firm is one of the five leaders (NACE 3-digit level)
Nestlé	38.8	13.1	412,413,414,417,421,423,428
Philip Morris	33.4	11.3	413,417,421,423,429
Unilever	26.7	14.6	411,412,414,415,421
ConAgra	24.8	-	-
Pepsico	19.1	-	-
Cargill	18.7	2.4	411
Coca-Cola	18.0	1.8	428
Danone	14.2	8.9	413,417,419,423,427,428
Archer Daniels	13.3	-	-
Mars	13.0	3.1	421,422
Grand Metropolitan	12.7	2.4	413,424
IBP	12.7	-	-
Kinn	11.6	-	-
CPC International	9.8	1.6	418,423
Anheuser-Busch	9.6	-	-
Sara Lee	9.4	1.3	423
ABF	9.2	-	416,418,419,420
Heinz	9.1	1.5	423
Asahi Breweries	9.1	-	-
Eridania Beghin-Say	9.1	-	-
Nabisco	8.3	-	-
Novartis	8.1	-	-
Cadbury-Schweppes	7.7	3.0	428
Campbell Soup	7.7	-	-
Guinness	7.6	2.2	424,427

Sources: AC Nielsen, *The Retail Pocket Book*, 1998; Davies, Rondi and Sembenelli (1998). Information is included in columns 2 and 3 (due to the nature of the source) only if a firm is a major supplier (in the top five) in at least one 3-digit industry.

of UK retailing). This is all suggestive of the fact that wholesaling generally lacks the very large independent operators which are commonly found in other areas of retailing on the one hand, and manufacturing on the other.

Turning to the food manufacturing sector, the EU is dominated by some of the world's leading multinational firms (see the next chapter). Nevertheless, it is argued that even these firms are losing bargaining muscle *vis-à-vis* the leading retailers with the latters' expansion in recent years. As testament to this, AIM (1995), for example, shows that the sales turnover of the EU's ten leading retailers far exceeds the fast moving consumer goods (FMCG) turnover of the EU's ten leading manufacturers. Although this is a striking statistic, it is misleading in at least two respects. First, necessarily, the turnover of a given retailer (A) buying exclusively from a given manufacturer (B) must always be greater simply because of the retail mark up – no matter how small. Second, even the most diversified food manufacturer does not supply the full range of food products carried by the retailer, and a more germane comparison of relative size should be conducted at a far less aggregated level than 'total food sales'. Such a disaggregated analysis will form part of the analysis in Chapter 7.

In anticipation, however, Table 6.12 reproduces a list of the world's leading 25 food and drink manufacturing firms and investigates their presence within the EU using an 'EU market share matrix for manufacturing' in 1993 (Davies, Rondi and Sembenelli, 1998). That matrix records the market shares of the five leading producers in each of the 15 '3-digit' food, drink and tobacco industries within EU manufacturing.

- Over half of the world's largest manufacturers have a leading presence in at least one manufacturing industry in the EU.[5] Even more strikingly, four firms in particular – Unilever, Nestlé, Philip Morris and Danone (BSN) – reappear frequently as the leaders in many individual product markets.

Clearly, any evaluation of the bargaining power of the two sides to the retailer-manufacturer relationship will need to recognise this considerable concentration on the manufacturing side as well.

6.6 CLASSIFYING MEMBER STATES

It is apparent, even from this brief overview, that significant differences exist between individual member states. One objective of this book is to examine how far these differences are being eroded and whether there is a discernible process of convergence. Notwithstanding possible convergence, however, we can categorise the member states into four broad groups:

- The UK, Germany and France tend to have the largest firms and stores, and concentration is high in spite of relatively large market size. A number of leading French and German firms are also increasingly multinational.
- Among the smaller northern member states — Sweden, Finland, Denmark and the Netherlands — concentration is again high (sometimes very high) and advanced retailing methods have achieved high penetration. On the other hand, these countries tend to be dominated by local indigenous firms which, while large relative to the market, are quite small in absolute terms.

The other two groups are rather more fluid and less well defined.

- Austria, Belgium (and perhaps Ireland) are smaller countries, strongly influenced by adjacent larger neighbours. Undoubtedly, these are less insular markets than those of the previous group, and Austria, in particular, has a strong German presence.
- In the southern member states — Italy, Portugal, Spain and Greece — traditional retailing structures are much more evident, and concentration is discernibly lower. However, generalisations for this group, in particular, may be dangerous. Certainly for Spain and Portugal, as various of the above tables reveal, change has been particularly rapid in very recent years (e.g. the fast diffusion of hypermarkets), partly the result of multinational expansion by leading firms from the first group. Moreover, Italy is an enigma. Not only is it obviously out of line with the three other large member states, but also there are (admittedly poorly documented) suggestions of a significant north-south heterogeneity within that country.

Quite obviously, while these groupings may be presentationally useful for some purposes, crude generalisations should generally be avoided.

NOTES

1. Two recent (seminal) examples are Sutton (1991) and Bresnahan and Reiss (1991).
2. Even acknowledging that there has been a genuine contraction in the number of outlets between these years, the difference between these two sources in the total number of food outlets in the EU as a whole (400 000, as opposed to nearly 900 000) is not credible. Also, different rankings for Germany between the two sources is disconcerting. This is a classic example of data inconsistencies and questions of reliability. Existing sources report wildly differing estimates of both the numbers of retail food outlets and the aggregate turnover of retailers in each member state. This derives from (i) familiar difficulties in defining small scale establishments, (ii) ambiguities in measuring turnover from food retailing, as opposed to the turnover of shops

selling (among other things) food. In general, the data appear to be more reliable at the aggregate retail level.
3. These include the fact that some estimates do not correct firms' turnovers for non-food sales, some include buying groups as single entities, and different conventions are used in counting the turnover of very small firms (which affect the denominator in this summary index.)
4. It is worth noting that most studies of private label sales record market shares even higher in Switzerland than in the UK. Switzerland is excluded from these comparisons as it is not a member of the EU.
5. In fact, the proportion may be even higher because the base list of the world's leading manufacturers involves some double counting, e.g. Nabisco appears separately from Nestlé.

7. The EU Retail Food Market Share Matrix

7.1 INTRODUCTION

This chapter builds on the overview of the previous chapter – which was based mainly on data and tabulations already in the public domain – by constructing a 'market share matrix for aggregate EU food retailing' for 1993 and 1996. The objective of this matrix[1] is to provide an integrated and harmonised database which contains most of the key information on the structure of the market and leading firms, but without being unmanageably large. Therefore, it focuses only on the main players. This keeps the matrix reasonably compact and easy to manipulate. (It would be easy to update as new data become available.) However, because of the concentrated nature of the market, this compactness is not at the expense of coverage – as will be seen, although the matrix includes only about 50 firms, they account for half of the entire turnover of food and daily goods retailing in the EU.

Section 7.2 presents the EU food retail market share matrix for 1996, and its counterpart for 1993. This provides an opening picture of the main features of structure and recent changes. The following sections each pursue the individual elements of structure in more detail. Section 7.3 examines aggregate concentration at the EU level, and Section 7.4 compares the concentration of sellers in each member state. Section 7.5 turns to the increasing extent of cross-border ('multinational') activity. Section 7.6 examines buyer concentration, by adjusting the estimates of seller concentration to allow for buying groups at the national level, and cross-border alliances at the aggregate EU level. Section 7.7 focuses more explicitly on the individual firms: it identifies the most prominent multinationals and discounters and constructs a league table of the leading firms by typical size of outlet. Section 7.8 switches attention on to the food manufacturing industries – presenting concentration ratios at both the EU levels and for individual member states, and listing the main multinational food producers.

7.2 THE EU RETAIL FOOD MARKET SHARE MATRIX

7.2.1 The Underlying Concept

As already mentioned, this stage of the statistical work is based on a newly constructed database which we refer to as the 'Market Share Matrix for Food Retailing in the EU'. This draws on a concept first used in previous work on the structure of manufacturing in the EU (Davies and Lyons et al., 1996). Its purpose is to provide a consistent mapping of some of the main features of the structure of this sector – both for the EU defined as a single entity, and for individual member states. In particular, it should include sufficient information to provide estimates of concentration of markets and the structure of the leading firms. However, emphasis is placed on confining data collection to manageable proportions, and, therefore, the database should be as compact and manageable as possible.

A basic requirement is that the matrix should include all of the major players on the EU stage. Thus, we start by identifying a set of leading firms, where a firm is defined as a leader if it satisfies one, or both, of two criteria:

- it is among the five leaders (largest firms) in at least one of the member states, and/or
- it is among the EU's largest 20 food retailers when judged by its aggregate EU food turnover.

In a fairly obvious sense then, a sample satisfying these criteria should include all firms with at least some significant degree of retail selling power at the EU or national level.

7.2.2 Constructing the Matrix

In order to make comparisons standardised, wherever possible, we have used a single source – the European Retail Handbook (C.I.R., 1998) – for our data on size. Company size is measured by the turnover of outlets devoted primarily to selling food, drink and tobacco. However, these outlets typically also sell other products (especially superstores and hypermarkets), and this can sometimes lead to unavoidable overestimates. On the other hand, we do not include the sales of these firms through non-food outlets such as DIY shops. Moreover, all estimates are confined to the firms' operations within the European Union (EU15).

Special attention has been paid to deriving comparable and consistent estimates of the size of the market (i.e. each member state's total retail food sales.) This is rarely discussed in much detail in most previous studies of market shares in the food retailing literature, and researchers often fail to document their sources. However, by deconstructing previous estimates, it appears that many are seriously flawed by a failure to compare like with like: sometimes, they define the market, in effect, as merely the sum of the turnovers of just the multiple grocers; sometimes, adjustments for non-food sales are made for some countries, but not for others. One manifestation of this is that different researchers have produced wildly different estimates of concentration for the same country (see Table 7.5 below for examples).

In constructing our own estimates of total market size, we have tried to be as encompassing as possible – including an allowance for the turnovers of specialists and traditional outlets, as well as those of the multiple grocers. We have used, as a starting point, the various time series magnitudes reported in the European Retail Handbook for 'Total Food, Drink and Tobacco Sales', most of which have been derived from official primary sources. However, these have also been scrutinised by comparing with macro aggregates (GDP, GDP per head and aggregate consumption) in order to ensure comparability, for example, on marginal and average propensities to consume retail food. For some countries (e.g. Benelux and Germany), this has caused us to revise upwards the published estimates of total market size. For this reason, our estimates of total market size are somewhat larger than those implicit in most previous studies; correspondingly, our estimates of concentration tend to be somewhat lower.

One other major difference from some previous studies is the exclusion, at this stage, of retail buying groups. More precisely, we do not assume that a buying group is a single seller (but see below for adjustments when turning to buyer concentration.)

7.2.3 The Matrix for 1996

Table 7.1 (a) reports the basic dimensions of the matrix for 1996. This is the most recent year for which comprehensive and consistent information is available across all firms and member states. (However, this does mean that some of our estimates are slightly out-of-date, especially in those member states in which there have been important mergers since 1996.)

The matrix covers the 15 member states in EU15 (but with Belgium and Luxembourg consolidated into a single entity). There are 56 firms on the matrix. Of these, 53 qualify by virtue of being one of the five leaders in at least one member state. In principle, 70 firms (5*14) could qualify under this criterion; however, eight firms occupy a leading position in more than one member state: Metro (6), Aldi (5), Promodès (3), Auchan (3), Carrefour (2), Rewe (2), Tesco (2), and Ahold (2).

These 56 firms include 17 of the 20 largest EU food retailers. The three other firms, Lidl & Schwarz, Casino and Spar Handels, have also been included under the second criterion – by virtue of their absolute size, they are among the EU's 20 largest food retailers even though they are not in the top five in any particular member state.

Table 7.1(a) The 1996 EU retail food market share matrix: broad dimensions

	Number	Sales (ecus bn)	Share of Retail Food (%)
Countries	14	-	-
Firms	56	379.5	49.7
Entries	113	-	-
Leading	70	334.2	43.7
Non-leading	43	45.4	5.9
Total EU Market Size	-	763.9	-

Source: See text.

In 1996, the aggregate turnover of these firms in food retailing in the EU amounted to 380 billion ecus – almost exactly half of the total turnover of food retailing in EU15. Of this, 334 billion ecus was accounted for by their 'leading' (i.e. top five) operations; this amounts to 43.7 per cent of total EU food retailing, and this is therefore the (weighted) average five firm concentration ratio in individual member states.

Table 7.1(b) shows the matrix in full. Reading down each column provides a picture of the upper tail of the size distribution for each member state; reading across each row reveals the pattern of each firm's multinational activities (where applicable). As can be seen, firms from Germany, France and the UK occupy all of the 17 top rankings. This reflects partly the size of the market in these three large countries, but it is also a manifestation of significant cross-border operations of some of these firms.

It should be stressed that the table is confined only to each firm's EU food retailing turnover. In some cases, this is significantly smaller than the firm's aggregate world turnover. This is for two reasons: (i) some firms have important non-food retailing activity within the EU (diversification), e.g. Sainsbury in DIY and Benetton in textiles; (ii) some have multinational food activities in the rest of the world, e.g. Ahold in the USA, and some of the German firms in Eastern Europe.

Table 7.1(b) The 1996 EU retail food market share matrix in full

	Firms:	Origin	A	BL	D	FIN	FRA	GER	GRE	IRE	IT	N	P	SP	SW	UK	TOTAL
1	Rewe	GER	3.5				0.1	21						0		0.5	25.3
2	Metro	GER	0.9	0	0.3		2	16	0.3		1.5	1.2	0.7	0.7			24.0
3	Aldi	GER	1.5	1.2	0.5		1	17				1.1				0.8	23.6
4	Promodès	FRA					16				1.3		0.3	5.1			23.4
5	Edeka	GER	0		0.2			20	0.2								20.6
6	Carrefour	FRA					16				0.5		0.3	3.7			20.4
7	Intermarché	FRA		0.2			19						0	0.1			19.7
8	Auchan	FRA		0			15				0.4		1	2.7			19.4
9	Tesco	UK								1						16	17.2
10	Leclerc	FRA	0.7				16						0.1	0.1			15.9
11	Tengelmann	GER						13			0.7	0.6					15.0
12	Sainsbury	UK														12	12.5
13	Lidl & Schwarz	GER		0			1.2	9.6			0.5		0	0.3		0.3	12.0
14	Casino	FRA					10										10.3
15	Spar Handels	GER						9									9.0
16	Asda	UK														8.5	8.5
17	Safeway	UK														8.1	8.1
18	Ahold	N										6.6	1.4				8.0

Turnover (bn ecus) in member state:

Rank	Company	Country							Total
19	Coop Italie	IT					6.7		6.71
20	ICA	SW						6.5	6.55
21	GIB group	BL	4.6			4.6			4.62
22	FDB Coop	D	4.6						4.57
23	Eroski	SP						3.3	3.30
24	Somerfield	UK						4	3.95
25	Spar Osterreich	A	2.5				1.1		3.57
26	Delhaize 'Le Lion'	BL	2.9	0.3					3.56
27	Dansk Supermk	D	2.7	0.4	0.3			0.4	3.43
28	Kesko	FIN	3.3						3.34
29	La Rinascente	IT					3.2		3.20
30	De Boer Unigro	N	0.3			1.9		0.5	2.83
31	KF Konsum	SW						2.8	2.75
32	D-Gruppen	SW	2.7					2.7	2.71
33	SOK	FIN	2.7						2.66
34	GS (Benetton)	IT					2.6		2.58
35	Vendex	N	0.4			2.1			2.45
36	Systembolaget	SW	2.3					2.4	2.35
37	Tuko	FIN							2.30
38	Esselunga	IT	1.7				1.7		1.74
39	Sonae	P						1.7	1.69
	(Promodès 22.5%)								

	Firm	Ctry														Total
40	Louis Delhaize	BL		1.6												1.61
41	ADEG	A	1.6													1.59
42	Colruyt	BL		1.5												1.52
43	Alko	FIN				1.4										1.42
44	Axel Johnson	SW													1.1	1.12
45	Dunnes	IRE											1.1	0		1.09
46	Dagrofa	D			1											1.01
47	Musgrave	IRE											1			0.97
48	Marinopoulos	GRE								0.8						0.83
49	Tradeka	FIN				0.8										0.82
50	Elomas	GRE								0.5						0.51
51	Centralkob	D			0.5											0.49
52	Veropoulos	GRE								0.5						0.48
53	Sklavenitis	GRE								0.4						0.44
54	BWG	IRE											0.4			0.41
55	Superquinn	IRE											0.4			0.41
56	Hipercor	SP												2.3		2.30
	Total matrix firms		11	13	9.8	11	98	107	3.1	3.9	20	14	5.5	19	15	380
	National market turnover		17	19	16	12	163	194	9.2	6	133	26	9	52	20	764
	Top 5		10	12	9.3	11	83	88	2.6	3.9	16	13	5	17	15	334
	CR5 (%)		59	62	59	89	51	45	28	64	12	50	56	32	78	43.7

7.2.4 The Matrix for 1993

All firms on the 1996 matrix have been tracked back to 1993, and the matrix has been re-constructed for that year by also taking into account any significant entry or exit between the two years. From the summary statistics (Table 7.2(a)), it can be seen that five more firms qualified for inclusion in 1993. The most notable exitors 1993–96 were Docks de France, Karl Wlaschek, Makro, and Power (ABF), each of which was acquired, and Konsum Osterreich, which collapsed.

Table 7.2(a) The 1993 EU retail food market share matrix: broad dimensions

	Number	Sales (ecus bn)	Share of Retail Food (%)
Countries	14	-	-
Firms	61	315.1	46.3
Entries	103	-	-
Leading	70	276.9	40.7
Non-leading	33	38.2	5.6
Total EU Market Size	-	681.2	-

Source: See text.

Although there were more firms on the 1993 matrix, they accounted for fewer non-zero cells and proportionately smaller aggregate turnover. As will be seen, this implies that both concentration and multinational activity have increased between these two years.

7.3 AGGREGATE CONCENTRATION AT THE EU LEVEL

Perhaps the most striking 'headline' from the matrix is that about 50 firms account for almost exactly half of the entire turnover of the EU food retail sector. This is a rough, 'first-blush', indication of the extent of concentration at the level of the EU, taken as a single entity.

However, it is only a crude measure which needs some refinement. In particular, we should remember that not all of the matrix firms are particularly large – especially in the lower tail, there are a number of quite small firms which qualify as leaders in the smaller member states. Therefore, it is more meaningful to concentrate only on the upper part of the matrix, remembering that, by construction, it includes the 20 largest food retailers.[2]

Table 7.2(b) The 1993 EU retail food market share matrix in full

			Turnover (bn ecus) in member state:													
			A	BL	D	FIN	FRA	GER	GRE	IRE	IT	N	P	SP	SW	UK	TOTAL
1	Edeka	Ger			0.49			20.5									20.9
2	Metro	Ger	1.02	0.16			1.84	16.5	0.1		1.24						20.8
3	Promodès	Fra					13.6	1.34	0.1		0.34			3.38			18.8
4	Leclerc	Fra					17.9							0			17.9
5	Aldi	Ger	1.06	0.97	0.39		0.21	13.9				0.9				0.23	17.6
6	Intermarché	Fra					17.0				0.1		0				17.1
7	Carrefour	Fra					12.3				0.1		0.24	2.97		0.2	15.8
8	Rewe	Ger						14.3									14.3
9	Tengelmann	Ger	0.51					10.2			0.55	0.46					11.7
10	Sainsbury	UK														11.7	11.7
11	Tesco	UK					0.5									10.9	11.4
12	Auchan	Fra					8.4				0.1			1.57			10.1
13	Casino	Fra					8.73										8.73
14	Safeway/Argyll	UK														7.28	7.28
15	Lidl & Schwarz	Ger					0.22	6.58			0		0				6.87
16	ICA	SW													6.73		6.73
17	Dock de France	Fra					6.25						0.38				6.63
18	Ahold	NL										6.12	0.5				6.62
19	Spar Handels	Ger						6.37									6.37

No.	Company	Country							Total
20	Asda	UK						6.24	6.24
21	Coop Italie	IT					5.94		5.94
22	GIB group	BL	4.48						4.48
23	Somerfield/Isosceles	UK						3.77	3.77
24	FDB Coop	D	3.7						3.7
25	Kesko	F	3.29						3.29
26	Standa	IT					2.89		2.89
27	Karl Wlaschek	A	2.49				0.1		2.59
28	KF Konsum(Coop)	SW						2.53	2.53
29	Systembolaget	SW						2.5	2.5
30	D-Gruppen	SW						2.5	2.5
31	Delhaize 'Le Lion'	BL	2.32	0.18					2.49
32	Spar Osterreich	A	1.91				0.29		2.21
33	SOK	F	2.13						2.13
34	Vendex	NL	0.18			1.83			2.01
35	La Rinascente	IT					2		2.00
36	Unigro	NL	0.45		0.28	1.25			1.98
37	Dansk Supermkt	D	1.8						1.80
38	Alko	F	1.74						1.74
39	GS	IT					1.61		1.61
40	Louis Delhaize	BL	1.56						1.56
41	Konsum Osterreich	A	1.53						1.53
42	Tuko	F	1.48						1.48

No.	Firm	Country															Total
43	Makro	NL										1.19	0.26				1.45
44	ADEG	A	1.41														1.41
45	Esselunga	IT									1.39						1.39
46	Axel Johnson	SW													1.11		1.11
47	Colruyt	BL		1.1													1.10
48	Power (ABF)	IRE								1.06							1.06
49	El Corte Inglés	SP												1.03			1.03
50	Sonae (Promodès)	P											1.01				1.01
51	Dagrofa	D			0.98												0.98
52	Dunnes	IRE								0.93							0.93
53	Musgrave	IRE								0.86							0.86
54	Pao de Acucar	P											0.74				0.74
55	Tradeka	F				0.54											0.54
56	Marinopoulos	Gre							0.35								0.35
57	Superquinn	IRE								0.25							0.25
58	BWG	IRE								0.19							0.19
59	Sklavenitis	Gre							0.19								0.19
60	Veropoulos	Gre							0.12								0.12
61	Centralkob	D			0.11												0.11
	Total all matrix firms		9.9	11.1	7.6	9.2	87.0	89.7	1.0	3.3	16.6	11.8	2.8	9.7	15.4	40.3	315.1
	National market turnover		15.5	17.3	13.6	9.8	146	167	8.2	5.3	127	21.5	7.5	43.2	19.4	79.3	681.2
	Top 5		8.4	10.4	7.4	9.2	69.6	75.4	0.9	3.3	13.8	11.3	2.7	9.3	15.4	39.9	276.9
	CR5 (%)		54.2	60.2	54.2	93.5	47.5	45.1	10.9	62.3	10.9	52.5	36.5	21.6	79.3	50.2	40.7

As shown in Table 7.3, the top ten firms account for 27.4 per cent of total EU retail food turnover, and the next ten for a further 12.6 per cent. Thus, the top 20 account for 40 per cent of total EU retail food activity. Superficially at least, this would appear to indicate a very high level of concentration in a sector which by its nature is geographically dispersed, and traditionally fragmented.

Table 7.3 Aggregate concentration in 1993 and 1996 (%)

	Cumulative Distribution of Aggregate Size	
Share of firms ranked:	1996	1993
1- 10	27.4	24.5
11-20	12.6	11.3
21-30	4.9	5.0
31-40	3.0	2.9
41-50	1.4	1.8
top 50	49.3	45.5

Source: Market share matrix.

However, in the absence of obvious comparators, 'high' has a somewhat empty ring to it – in what sense is 40 per cent high? And compared to what? First, it is certainly high relative to the share of the top 20 firms in EU manufacturing: according to Davies and Lyons et al. (1998), the top 20 in the manufacturing sector accounted for only 14.5 per cent of sales in 1993. Second, and on the other hand, it does not appear to be as high as reported concentration in the US retail food sector. According to estimates attributed to the Harvard Business School, and reported in *Food Business News*, July 1998, the top ten in the US account for 37 per cent of total US retail food turnover (i.e. about ten percentage points more than our figure for the EU.)

In truth, however, neither of these comparisons is particularly illuminating. After all, manufacturing is much larger, and a more heterogeneous sector than retail food, and it is hardly surprising that it records lower concentration. Similarly, a comparison with the US retail food sector might also be misleading: first, we are not confident that the above quoted US estimate is based on a measure of total market size (the denominator) which is as broad-based as the one we have used for the EU; second, there is perhaps no reason for expecting the EU to be similar to the US, at least at this stage in European integration.

Ultimately, the most important comparison is inter-temporal – how is aggregate EU retail food concentration changing over time? Unfortunately, here, we are confined to just a comparison of our own estimates for 1993 and 1996. Nevertheless, even over this relatively short period, there appears to have been a significant increase in EU concentration. As shown in Table 7.3, there was an increase of 4.2 percentage points in the share of the top 20 firms between 1993 and 1996. Moreover, the table reveals that the increased share of matrix firms is almost entirely attributable to the top 20 firms. Indeed, the next 30 actually suffered a joint loss of 0.4 percentage points between the two years. This is due, in part, to the rapid growth of the very largest firms, internally and by merger, and the corresponding exit of some important medium-large firms, as described in Section 7.2.4.

7.4 CONCENTRATION WITHIN INDIVIDUAL MEMBER STATES

Tables 7.4 to 7.6 turn the spotlight on to concentration within individual member states. Table 7.4 confirms that the increase in concentration at the EU level is mirrored by typically increasing concentration in the individual member states – by about three percentage points on average between 1993 and 1996.

Table 7.4 Five firm national concentration ratios in 1993 and 1996 (%)

	1996	1993
Austria	59	54
Belgium/Lux	62	60
Denmark	59	54
Finland	89	94
France	51	48
Germany	45	45
Greece	28	11
Ireland	64	62
Italy	12	11
Netherlands	50	52
Portugal	56	36
Spain	32	22
Sweden	78	79
UK	56	50

Source: Market share matrix.

It also confirms important differences between member states. Broadly speaking, the ranking of member states is as described in the previous chapter. The highest five firm concentration ratios are to be found in Finland and Sweden, and the lowest in the southern countries – Greece, Spain, Italy. The UK, France and Germany lie within the middle of the range. Perhaps most interestingly, there appear to have been significant increases in concentration in Portugal, Spain, Austria, Greece and the UK. Moreover, since these estimates refer to 1996, they will not reflect the effects of continued merger activity post-1996 in Spain, Portugal and the Netherlands in particular. In those countries, concentration is probably now higher than shown in the table.

As a reference point, Table 7.5 digresses briefly by comparing our estimates with those from previous studies. As can be seen, our estimates are typically lower – by about ten percentage points on average.[3]

Table 7.5 Comparisons of CR5 from different sources

	Our estimates 1996	LDA 1997	PBUK 1996	EH 1996	AIM 1992	HBS	OXIRM 1996	Average of other estimates
Austria	58.6	79	67.9	72.9				73.3
Bel/Lux	61.6	57	56.9	77.4	53	60		60.9
Denmark	59.5		48.0			78		63.0
Finland	89.1	96	95.4	97.5				96.3
France	50.6	67.2	60.1		49	65		60.3
Germany	45.4	75.2	41.5	73.5	37			56.8
Greece	28.0		58.7					58.7
Ireland	64.2	50	50.4					50.2
Italy	11.8	30	35.0			21	58.5	36.1
Netherlands	50.4	79	76.7	71.7	59			71.6
Portugal	55.7	52	52.9				55.0	53.3
Spain	32.1	38	34.6		23		47.7	35.8
Sweden	77.9	87	70.5	93.5				83.7
UK	56.2	67	65.2		60	63		63.8
Average	52.9							61.7

Sources: La Distribution Alimentaire; AIM; PBUK, UK Pocketbook; EH, European Handbook; OXIRM, referred to in 'Food Retailing in Southern European Countries', European Regional Review, 1998; HBS, Harvard Business School (date not reported).

Tables 7.6 and 7.7 have a more substantive role. They delve behind the simple CR5 summary statistics. Table 7.6 identifies the magnitude of size inequalities among the top five firms within each country. Using the typology defined in the notes to the table, certain stylised facts emerge:

- in four of the smaller northern member states – Belgium, Denmark, the Netherlands and Sweden – the leading firm is 'dominant' in the sense that it accounts for one quarter of the market (or more), and is faced with only much smaller rivals.

Table 7.6 A typology of market structures based on market shares among the top five

	CR5	MS1	MS2	MS3	MS4	MS5	
Austria	58.6	20.5	14.5	9.3	9.0	5.2	duopoly
Belgium/Lux	61.6	24.0	15.2	8.3	7.9	6.1	dominant firm
Denmark	59.5	29.2	17.3	6.4	3.4	3.1	dominant firm
Finland	89.1	28.3	22.5	19.4	12.0	7.0	triopoly
France	50.6	11.9	10.1	9.7	9.6	9.4	symmetric oligopoly
Germany	45.4	10.9	10.5	8.9	8.4	6.7	symmetric oligopoly
Greece	28.0	9.0	5.6	5.2	4.8	3.4	unconcentrated
Ireland	64.2	17.9	16.6	16.2	6.7	6.7	triopoly
Italy	11.8	5.1	2.4	1.9	1.3	1.1	unconcentrated
Netherlands	50.4	25.7	8.0	7.6	4.7	4.4	dominant firm
Portugal	55.7	18.7	14.9	11.1	7.6	3.4	triopoly
Spain	32.1	10.0	8.6	7.1	5.0	1.4	unconcentrated
Sweden	77.9	33.0	13.8	13.7	11.8	5.6	dominant firm
UK	56.2	18.5	14.2	9.7	9.3	4.5	duopoly
Average	52.9	18.8	12.5	9.6	7.3	4.9	

Notes: Definitions (based on identifying the 'natural breaks' within the top five). Dominant Firm: MS1>20 per cent and MS1>1.5*MS2; Duopoly: MS2>12.5 per cent and MS2>1.5*MS3 but not dominant firm; Triopoly: MS3>10 per cent and MS3>1.5*MS4, but not dominant firm or duopoly; Symmetric oligopoly: none of the above; each firm is 'sizeable' (MS>8 per cent), and at least 67 per cent the size of its immediate, higher ranked, neighbour; Unconcentrated: No firm has MS>10 per cent, and CR5<33 per cent.

Source: Market share matrix.

Table 7.7 Major mergers and acquisitions since 1992

Country	Year	Acquiring firm		Acquired firm	
		Name	*Status*	*Name*	*Status*
AUSTRIA	1996	Rewe (GER)	MNE entry	Billa (from Karl Wlaschek)	#1
	1998	Rewe (GER)	#1	J. Meinl	#6
	1998	Edeka (GER)	MNE entry	Adeg	#3
BELGIUM	1995	Promodès (F)	MNE entry	Mestdagh (25% stake)	top 10
DENMARK	1997	FDB	#1	NKL/KF	
FINLAND	1996	Kesko	#1	Tuko (not allowed by EC)	#3
FRANCE	1992	Tesco (UK)	MNE entry	Catteau	top 20
	1994	Delhaize 'Le Lion' (BL)	MNE entry	PG	top 20
	1996	Auchan	#5	Docks de France	#6
	1997	Promodès	#3	Casino (contested, did not occur)	top 10
	1997	Carrefour	#2	Cora (increased holding)	#7
	1997	Casino	#6	Leader Price	top 20
	1997	Promodès	#3	Catteau (ex Tesco)	top 20
	1997	Comptoirs Modernes	#8	PG (ex Delhaize 'Le Lion')	top 20
	1997	Casino	#6	Franprix	top 20
	1998	Carrefour	#2	Comptoirs Modernes	#8
GERMANY	1992	Metro	#4	ASKO	#6
	1997	ITM/ Intermarché (F)	MNE entry	Spar Handels	#6
	1997	Spar Handels	#6	Pro Verbraucher	top 30
	1998	Metro	#4	Alkauf	top 10
	1998	Walmart (US)	MNE entry	Wertkauf	top 20
	1998	Spar Handels	#6	Pfamkuch	top 30

Country	Year	Acquiring firm		Acquired firm	
GREECE	1992	Delhaize 'Le Lion' (BL)	MNE entry	Alfa Beta	top 10
	1995	Promodès (F)	MNE entry	Marinopoulos (20% hldg)	#1
IRELAND	1997	Tesco (UK)	MNE entry	Power (acq from ABF)	#2
ITALY	1993	Carrefour (F)	#3	Gran Sole	top 20
	1995	La Rinascente	MNE entry	CEDIS	top 20
	1996	Promodès (F)	MNE entry	Garosci (joint venture)	top 10
	1997	Promodès (F)	MNE entry	GS (acquired a holding)	#5
	1997	Auchan/Leroy (F)	MNE entry	La Rinascente (JV)	#3
	1998	Tengelmann (GER)	MNE entry	Gruppo PAM	top 10
	1998	La Rinascente -Auchan	#/1	Colmark	n.a.
NETHERLANDS	1992	Ahold	#1	Schuitema	#10
	1997	Metro (GER)	MNE entry	Makro-SHV	#10
	1997	De Boer	#4	Unigro (merger)	#4
	1998	Vendex-De Boer Unigro	#3	KBB	#10
	1998	Vendex	#3	Bijenkorf	n.a.
	1998	Vendex	#3	De Boer Unigro	#4
PORTUGAL	1992	Ahold (NL)	MNE entry	Jeronimo Martins (49%)	#2
	1997	Promodès (F)	#1	Lojas de Desconto	top 10
	1997	Pao (Auchan) (F)	#3	Minipreco	top 10
SPAIN	1997	Promodès (F)	#1	Simago	top 20
	1998	Gidae	#4	Merger: Eroski (#4), Unide (#8) Syp	top 10
	1998	Alcampo	#5	Sabeco	top 10
UK	1993	Rewe (GER)	MNE entry	Budgens	top 20
	1998	Somerfield	#6	Kwik Save	#5

Notes: Acquiring firm: shows the firm's ranking by market share in the country concerned or if used the acquisition for multinational entry. Acquired firm: shows the firm's ranking by market share in the country at the time of acquisition; 'top ten' ('top 20') indicates in the top ten (or 20) at the time of acquisition.

- in three of the southern member states – Italy, Spain and Greece – not only is concentration relatively low, but also even the largest firm has a limited market share (ten per cent or less). These appear to be unconcentrated markets by any criterion, although recent merger activity suggests that the picture is currently changing in Spain.

In the remaining seven countries, concentration is higher and involves two or more roughly equally sized firms:

- Germany and France both display structures in which all top five firms have sizeable, and roughly comparable, market shares.
- in the UK, also, four firms have market shares in the region of ten per cent or more, although, in this case, two – Tesco and Sainsbury – are significantly larger than the other two.[4]
- in each of Austria, Finland, Ireland and Portugal, there are two or three firms significantly larger than the other leaders. Loosely speaking, they can be characterised as duopolies or triopolies.

Although speculative, the make-up of the groups just identified is, arguably, more revealing than concentration ratios in identifying the nature of the underlying size of market/concentration relationship – and in predicting where change is most likely in the future. Broadly speaking, two speculative hypotheses might be put forward.

H1: There is a long-run equilibrium relationship in which the size of national market will determine the number of significant players. In smaller member states, the market may only be able to sustain one or two major firms, while, in the larger countries it may sustain as many as four or five firms.

H2: This equilibrium may be near to current reality in some countries: Germany, France, the UK, Austria, Benelux, Sweden and Denmark. In others, however, it remains to be achieved: Greece, Italy, Spain, Finland, Ireland and Portugal.

This is, of course, highly speculative, but there are certainly signs of intensive recent merger activity in most of the second set of countries listed under H2. If our hypothesis is correct, concentration should increase in all but Finland; and, we might expect perhaps three leaders to break away from the pack in Italy and Spain. In each of Ireland, Portugal and Finland, however, it may be that in the long run, only one or two major players will survive.

If such restructuring is to occur, mergers and acquisitions will clearly play a major role. Table 7.7 lists the main mergers and acquisitions of recent years, arranged by member state and annotated by the status of the acquiring and acquired firms. Two more or less general trends are apparent across the member states. First, there has been significant cross-border (multinational) entry. While of itself this does not necessarily increase concentration in the member state concerned in the short run, the longer-run ramifications and subsequent developments may well increase concentration. For example, the acquisition by Rewe of Billa from Karl Wlaschek in Austria merely changed the ownership of one of the market leaders initially. Subsequently, however, there are signs of further German entry into Austria, leading to continued consolidation and concentration. The second general trend is that the acquiring firms shown tend to have a market ranking within the top five, while the acquired firms tend to have come from the middle part of the country size distribution (i.e. often outside the top five, but within the top ten or top 20.) This mirrors the development noted above, at the level of the EU as a whole, for the very largest firms to expand at the expense of their medium-sized rivals.

Turning to differences between the member states, the table points to major activity in some of the smaller and/or southern states in which we have already suggested major restructuring is likely (e.g. Portugal, Italy, Spain, Netherlands). In addition, however, there have been major waves of mergers in the last few years in both France and Germany, but not the UK. In the UK, rumours and tentative merger proposals among the leading firms have been a common feature in recent years, but so far little has materialised beyond the recent merger of Somerfield and Kwik Save (ranked respectively five and six by turnover in the UK).[5]

Finally, Table 7.8 places these data in a chronological perspective, from which it appears that significant merger activity has intensified in the mid- to late 1990s.

Table 7.8 Annual time series of major M&A activity

Year	Number of mergers
1992	5
1993	2
1994	1
1995	3
1996	4
1997	17
1998	16
Total	48

Source: See text.

Table 7.9(a) Cross-border operations by member state in 1996

Firms' turnover (bn ecus) in:

Country of origin	A	BL	D	FIN	FRA	GER	GRE	IRE	IT	NETH	P	SP	SW	UK	Total
Austria	4.1								1.1						5.2
Bel/Lux		10.7			0.3		0.3								11.3
Denmark			8.8			0.4								0.4	9.5
Finland				10.6											10.6
France		0.2			92.9		0.2		2.2		1.7	11.8			109.0
Germany	6.7	1.3	1.0		4.3	106.8	0.3		2.7	2.9	0.7	1.2		1.6	129.5
Greece							2.3								2.3
Ireland								2.9							2.9
Italy									14.2						14.2
Netherlands		0.7								10.6	1.4	0.5			13.2
Portugal											1.7				1.7
Spain												4.5			4.5
Sweden													15.5		15.5
UK								1.0						49.3	50.3
Total	10.8	12.9	9.8	10.6	97.5	107.2	3.1	3.9	20.2	13.5	5.5	18.0	15.5	51.2	379.5

Source: Market share matrix.

Table 7.9(b) *Cross-border operations by member state in 1993*

Country of origin	Firms' turnover (bn ecus) in:															
	A	BL	D	FIN	FRA	GER	GRE	IRE	IT	NETH	P	SP	SW	UK	Total
Austria	7.3								0.4						7.7
Bel/Lux		9.5					0.2								9.6
Denmark			6.6												6.6
Finland				9.2											9.2
France					84.2	1.3	0.1		0.6		0.3	8.3		0.2	95.1
Germany	2.6	1.0	1.0		2.3	88.3	0.1		1.8	1.4				0.2	98.8
Greece							0.7								0.7
Ireland								3.3							3.3
Italy									13.8						13.8
Netherlands		0.6								10.4	0.8	0.3			12.07
Portugal											1.8				1.8
Spain												1.0			1.0
Sweden													15.4		15.4
UK					0.5									39.9	40.4
Total	9.9	11.1	7.6	9.2	87.0	89.7	1.0	3.3	16.6	11.8	2.8	9.7	15.4	40.3	315.2

Source: Market share matrix.

7.5 CROSS-BORDER OPERATIONS

One of the most attractive features of the market share matrix is that it provides a very clear integrated picture of the flows of cross-border activities by Europe's leading firms.[6] In the three parts to Table 7.9, the firm level data in the full matrix have been consolidated into country aggregates. For example, reading across the row for Germany, we have a picture of the activity of the German market leaders across the other member states, as well as in Germany itself. Reading down the column for Germany, the numbers refer to (the much smaller) operations of firms from other countries in Germany.[7] Conceptually, this is analogous to a matrix of intra-EU FDI flows arising from foreign investment, both inward and outward, between member states.

Table 7.9(c) Cross-border operations by member state: summary table

	1996			1993		
	Domestic	In	Out	Domestic	In	Out
Austria	4.1	6.7	1.1	7.3	2.6	0.4
Bel/Lux	10.7	2.2	0.6	9.5	1.6	0.2
Denmark	8.76	1.0	0.7	6.6	1.0	-
Finland	10.6	-	-	9.2	-	-
France	92.9	4.6	16.1	84.2	2.8	10.9
Germany	107.0	0.2	22.5	88.3	1.4	10.5
Greece	2.3	0.8	-	0.7	0.3	-
Ireland	2.9	1.0	-	3.3	-	-
Italy	14.2	6.0	-	13.8	2.8	-
Netherlands	10.6	2.9	2.6	10.4	1.4	1.7
Portugal	1.7	3.8	-	1.8	1.0	-
Spain	4.5	13.5	-	1.0	8.6	-
Sweden	15.5	-	-	15.4	-	-
UK	49.3	1.9	1.0	39.9	0.4	0.5
Total	335.1	44.5	44.5	291.3	23.9	23.9

Note: 'dom' (for domestic) indicates turnover of firms originating from a member state; 'in' indicates turnover of firms from other member states; 'out' indicates turnover of firms originating from other member states.

As can be seen from Table 7.9(a), the majority of overseas activity in 1996 originated from Germany and France, with smaller magnitudes attributable to the Benelux countries, the Netherlands, the UK, Austria and Denmark (only one firm in each of the latter three countries is involved.) In terms of the received theory of multinational firms, this activity by firms from the smaller member states can be explained by a desire to break free from the constraints on growth implied by a limited home market. However, much more important is the explanation of why German and French (but not UK) firms have been so active in cross-border activity. Again, this may be due, in part, to constraints on domestic growth – remembering that in these two countries, there are at least five strong market leaders vying for market share. In addition, however, this cross-border expansion may be motivated by a desire to exploit firm-specific assets, including new selling modes and structures (for example, discounting). Turning to the distribution across the host countries (inward), it is clear that the major recipients of inward FDI are the southern and smaller member states. Significantly, Sweden and Finland stand alone, with no linkages, outwards or inwards, to the rest of the matrix.

Part (b) of the table replicates the analysis for 1993. This reveals how quickly the non-diagonal elements of the matrix have changed in just three years. Part (c) of the table merely summarises, by comparing the outward and inward aggregates for each country. Perhaps the key statistics here are to be found in the final row. In 1996, 44.5 bn ecus of the turnover of matrix firms was accounted for by their operations outside their home member states. This amounts to 11.7 per cent of the matrix total, and compares with only 7.5 per cent in 1993. In this sense, cross-border activity has increased in proportionate terms by over 50 per cent.

7.6 IMPACT OF BUYING GROUPS: BUYER VERSUS SELLER CONCENTRATION

Thus far, we have been concerned with retailer seller concentration and, as such, it is appropriate not to conceive of the buying group as a single entity. However, when measuring buyer power (*vis-à-vis* food manufacturers), it is arguably appropriate to group together all firms buying through a single purchasing arm.

Assuming all identified buying groups can be treated in this way, Table 7.10 revises the previous estimates of seller concentration, by including any buying group whose firms have a joint market share which places them in the top five.[8] As can be seen, such adjustments must be made for eight of the member states and, in each case, the effect is to increase significantly, sometimes drastically (e.g. France) the value of CR5. The average across member states now increases by ten percentage points to over 60 per cent, and only Greece and Italy lie significantly below 50 per cent.

Moving beyond buying groups which operate within individual member states, Table 7.11 turns to the cross-border alliances. This shows the constituent members of each alliance and their aggregate turnover. Nearly all of the firms on the matrix belong to one or another of these alliances. The largest appears to be AMS, whose members have a combined turnover of 65 bn ecus, which is about 8.5 per cent of the total EU market. The joint turnover of the eight alliances listed amounts to over 250 bn ecus, i.e. roughly one third of the total EU market.

Table 7.10 Five firm concentration ratios adjusted for buying groups, 1996

	Excl. BG	Incl. BG	Buying groups in top five
Austria	58.6	58.6	
Belgium/Lux	61.6	84.6	BLOC, VAC
Denmark	59.5	76.6	SuperVib
Finland	89.1	89.1	
France	50.6	78.2	Cometca, Leclerc, ITM, Centrale Casino, Eurocham
Germany	45.4	50.0	Markant
Greece	28.0	28.0	
Ireland	64.2	64.2	
Italy	11.8	26.2	ADI, Euromadis, Intermedia, Supercentrale
Netherlands	50.4	69.6	SuperUnie, KBB, Radar
Portugal	55.7	62.4	Uniarme, Elos
Spain	32.1	49.3	Euromadi, IFA
Sweden	77.9	77.9	
UK	56.2	56.2	
Average	52.9	62.2	

Note: 'excl. BG' means excluding buying groups; 'incl. BG' means including buying groups.

7.7 FIRM-SPECIFIC ANALYSIS

Tables 7.12 to 7.14 document three aspects of the structure of individual firms. The 18 firms listed in Table 7.12 account for virtually all the cross-border activities depicted earlier in Table 7.9. The two indices shown each indicate the relative importance to the firm of its operations outside its own member state. For example, 32 per cent of Metro's turnover emanates from its non-German food operations and the E value (an entropy index) indicates how widely dispersed the turnover is across different locations.[9] Unsurprisingly, given earlier tables, the list is dominated by firms from Germany, France and the Benelux countries.

Similarly, the make-up of the list of leading discounters, shown in Table 7.13, comes as little surprise. It is dominated by four of the largest German firms, followed by Promodès. Together, these five firms operate about 15,000

Table 7.11 Cross-border alliances

Alliance Members:		Combined turnover (bn ecus)
AMS		64.93
Ahold	Hakon Gruppen	
Safeway	Jeronimo Martins	
ICA	Mercadona	
Kesko	Rinascente	
Edeka	Superquinn	
Allkauf	Casino	
EMD		53.71
Musgrave	Selex	
Syntrade	Euromadi	
DAGAB-UNIL	Uniarme	
Supervib	UNIL	
Markant	ZEV Markant	
Nisa Todays	Leclerc	
DEURO		44.37
Makro	Metro	
Carrefour	plus NAF International	
NAF INT		20.31
Coop Italia	NKL	
Coop S. H.	FDB	
KF Gruppen	CWS UK	
S-Group	Tradeka	
EUROGROUP		27.75
Coop Schweiz	Vendex-De Boer Unigro	
Markant	Rewe-Billa	
SED		17.78
Esselunga	Sainsbury	
Delhaize 'Le Lion'		
BIGS		14.43
Hellaspar	Bernag Ovag	
BWG/Spar	Dagrofa	
Tukospar	Spar Landmark	
Spar	Unidis (De Boer Unigro)	
Despar		
EUROPARTNERS		11.21
Superunie	Cora-Louis Delhaize	
Somerfield		

Note: Turnover is estimated for EU member states. Most EMD members are national buying groups.

Table 7.12 The leading multinational firms

		% outside home MS	E index	Also operates in:
Metro	Ger	32.1	3.51	France, Italy, Netherlands, Austria, Spain, Portugal, Greece, Denmark, Belgium
De Boer Unigro	NL	31.4	2.30	Spain, Belgium
Spar Osterreich	A	30.0	1.84	Italy
Promodès	Fra	29.8	2.30	Spain, Portugal, Italy, Greece
Aldi	Ger	26.3	2.81	Austria, Belgium, Denmark, France, Netherlands, UK.
Carrefour	Fra	22.2	1.93	Spain, Italy, Portugal
Dansk Supermkt	D	21.2	1.94	Germany, UK
Auchan	Fra	20.8	2.00	Spain, Portugal, Italy, Belgium/Luxembourg
Lidl and Schwarz	Ger	19.7	2.15	France, Italy, Spain, UK, Belgium, Portugal
Delhaize 'Le Lion'	BL	17.9	1.81	France, Greece
Ahold	NL	17.0	1.58	Portugal
Rewe	Ger	16.4	1.70	Austria, UK, France, Spain
Vendex	NL	16.1	1.55	Belgium
Tengelmann	Ger	13.6	1.76	Italy, Netherlands, Austria, Spain
Tesco	UK	5.8	1.25	Ireland
Intermarché	Fra	1.8	1.11	Belgium, Spain, Portugal
Dunnes	IRE	1.7	1.09	Spain
Leclerc	Fra	1.3	1.08	Spain, Portugal
Edeka	Ger	1.1	1.06	Denmark, Austria

Note: '% outside home MS' is the percentage of firm turnover accounted for by operations outside its home member state. The E index is an entropy index of multinationality, expressed in number equivalent form. Its lower limit is one (scored by a firm operating exclusively in its home member state) and higher values indicate greater dispersion across member states. For example, Metro's operations are equivalent to a firm operating in equal proportions in 3.5 different member states.

discount outlets, which is roughly 60 per cent of the total within the EU. Significantly, each of these firms is multinational in its discounting operations. In terms of the conventional theory of multinational firms, their specific asset appears to be their expertise in the discounting selling mode.

Table 7.13 *The leading discounters*

									Number of outlets in member state:						
Member states: Firms:	A	BL	D	FIN	FRA	GER	GRE	IRE	IT	N	P	SP	SW	UK	Total
Aldi	197	280	177		320	2775				327				176	4252
Lidl and Schwarz		45			585	2017			195		19	130		132	3123
Tengelmann	Some					2660			120	Some		40			2820+
Rewe	Some				60	2393			70			30			2553+
Promodès					28				Some		125	1727			1880+
Dansk Supermkt			237			126								106	469
Carrefour					346										346
Casino					241										241
Vendex		52								160					212
FDB Coop			211												211
SOK				210											210
Intermarché					207										207
Tuko				145											145
Louis Delhaize		144													144
Auchan											124				124

															Total
Coop Italie									100						100
Marinopoulos							100								100
ICA													81		81
KF Konsum													57		57
Delhaize Le Lion	51														51
Tesco								18							18
La Rinascente									7						7
GS (Benetton)									Some						0+
Metro						Some									0+
Other firms	371	190	114	465	153	2159	n.a.	n.a.	1868	120	46	388	167	926	6645
Total number of discount stores	568	762	739	820	1940	1213	n.a.	n.a.	2360	607	314	2315	305	1440	24300
% of turnover accounted for	17	25	20	12	7	30	n.a.	n.a.	10	13	9	9	11	11	

Note: In some cases multinational presence was known but the number of outlets was not known. These are indicated by 'some' in the table and a + sign is included in the final column.

Table 7.14 Firms with the largest scale outlets

	Average turnover per outlet (mn ecus)
Asda	39.9
Sainsbury	33.0
Leclerc	30.7
Tesco	26.7
Superquinn	25.3
Carrefour	24.7
Sonae (Promodès 22.5%)	23.8
Esselunga	20.4
Dunnes	18.9
Safeway	16.6
Auchan	15.9
Metro	15.4
Sklavenitis	14.3
Colruyt	10.9
Marinopoulos	8.3
Intermarché	8.2
Delhaize 'Le Lion'	8.1
GIB group	7.0
La Rinascente	6.9
Somerfield	6.6
Axel Johnson	6.3
Eroski	6.2
Systembolaget	6.2
GS (Benetton)	6.1
Aldi	5.5
Dansk Supermkt	5.5
Coop Italie	5.3
Alko	5.1
Promodès	4.7
SOK	4.6
Ahold	4.1
Average for all matrix firms	4.1

Turning to the typical size of outlet operated by firms, Table 7.14 provides the one instance in which UK firms dominate the rankings. Judged by these data, the UK market leaders tend to operate shops which are as much as eight times larger than the average for all firms on the matrix. This indicator may be biased if there are important inter-country differences in the way that the number of outlets is measured. On the face of it, however, this indicator is consistent with the view that shopping is a more scale-intensive activity in the UK. The table also shows that French hypermarket chains, such as Leclerc and Carrefour, also have a high level of turnover per outlet as one might expect.

7.8 THE STRUCTURE OF FOOD MANUFACTURING

Finally, Table 7.15 records some summary statistics on the industries manufacturing food and other daily goods. These data are derived from the EU manufacturing market share matrix (Davies and Lyons et al., 1998), EUROSTAT trade data and national production censuses. It complements Table 6.12 of the previous chapter, which identified some of the leading multinational manufacturing firms involved. The main features of these data are as follows:

- At the EU level, the five firm concentration ratio in the typical 3-digit food manufacturing industry is about 30 per cent. This compares to CR5 of 15 per cent from the EU retail matrix. In some sectors, e.g. tobacco, confectionery, and soaps and detergents, it exceeds 40 per cent. Broadly speaking, manufacturing concentration tends to be higher where the products are typically advertising-intensive with pronounced brand loyalty.
- Concentration has tended to increase, 1987–93, by about two percentage points on average. This rate of increase, and the absolute levels, are both somewhat larger than the averages for all manufacturing industries over this period.
- Typically, intra-EU trade flows are relatively small in these industries: about 15 per cent of EU consumption is accounted for by imports from elsewhere in the EU. This compares with an average of 23 percent for all manufactured goods. By far the most important product is domestic and office chemicals where nearly 50 per cent of consumption is sourced from intra-EU trade, followed at some distance by fruit and vegetables, and fish products.
- Multinational production within the EU is higher than for manufacturing as a whole, and it increased quite dramatically between 1987 and 1993. Multinationality increased markedly in products such as oils and fats, spirits, wine and beer and, apparently, by a very large amount in starch products. High degrees of multinationality occur in soaps and detergents, oils and fats, starch, confectionery and other foods.
- Comprehensive consistent data on concentration in the individual member states is less readily available. The estimates for the four countries shown in Table 7.15 indicate typical CR5 values in the region

Table 7.15 *The structure of EU manufacturing: food and other daily good '3-digit' industries*

Five firm concentration ratios

	NACE	EU		France		UK		Belgium		Germany		Intra-EU Trade		MNE	
		93	87	92	85	92	86	91	86	93	87	93	87	93	87
PHARMACEUTICALS	257	20	22	12	11	44	38	47	51	25	26	14	12	3.4	2.9
SOAP & DETERGENTS DOMESTIC AND	258	43	34	25	27	59	46	55	52	50	33	16	11	5.4	4.3
OFFICE CHEMICALS	259	52	62	75	66	58	48	62	85	65	66	49	48	1.9	1.8
OILS & FATS	411	39	29	53	64	53	73	84	85	50	53	12	13	4.1	2.8
MEAT PRODUCTS	412	5.6	6.5	7.4	6.3	20	20	11	10	28	24	19	20	2	1.9
DAIRY PRODUCTS	413	18	15	14	15	59	59	28	33	24	17	17	15	3.4	2.7
FRUIT & VEG PRODUCTS	414	15	16	20	26	47	33	39	43	31	28	27	29	2.9	2.6
FISH PRODUCTS	415	22	17	30	20	49	63	75	73	58	48	21	19	1.7	1.2
GRAIN MILLING	416	17	22	23	24	62	69	39	33	36	35	5.1	8.5	1.0	1.0
PASTA	417	30	24	79	79	n.a.	n.a.	87	89	70	76	12	7.2	1.6	1.3
STARCH	418	61	40	96	95	n.a.	n.a.	98	100	n.a.	n.a.	16	14	4.8	1.3
BREAD & BISCUITS	419	20	23	7.1	8.4	47	55	22	25	15	10	8.3	6.9	1.7	1.3

SUGAR	420	40	31	56	67	100	100	89	74	86	65	8.1	5.2	1.3	1.3
CONFECTIONERY	421	47	39	33	43	70	61	41	40	38	31	18	15	4.1	3.4
ANIMAL FOODS	422	13	15	20	15	54	50	37	40	36	38	9.3	6.2	1.6	1.3
OTHER FOODS	423	22	21	42	25	30	29	39	45	42	39	14	12	3.9	2.9
DISTILLING	424	32	37	29	33	63	64	47	56	40	39	20	15	2.8	1.7
WINE & CIDER	426	18	18	21	27	91	92	96	98	62	58	14	14	2.0	1.3
BEER	427	25	26	71	55	50	50	59	46	18	14	5.4	3.9	2.5	1.7
SOFT DRINKS	428	36	30	47	46	63	37	58	57	24	21	5.3	4.3	2.5	2.4
TOBACCO	429	49	55	100	100	100	99	94	92	89	89	7.7	6	1.5	1.1
Average of above		29.7	27.7	40.9	40.5	58.8	57.1	57.4	58.2	44.4	41.5	15.2	13.6	2.7	2.0
Average for all manufacturing		25.7	24.8									23.2	21.0	1.3	1.8

Notes: 'Intra-EU trade' denotes the ratio of intra-EU trade to consumption (expressed as a percentage); 'MNE' denotes the average entropy index of multinationality among the five EU market leaders in the industry concerned: the lowest value is one, where none of the top five firms is multinational – higher values indicate greater dispersion of output across the member states.

Source: Davies et al. (1998).

of 40–60 per cent, with the UK and Belgium tending to have more concentrated industries than France and Germany.

Obviously, there are important inter-industry differences. Nevertheless, the stylised picture is one in which concentration at the EU level tends to be higher on the manufacturing side than in retailing. On the other hand, levels seem roughly comparable at the national level. Trade flows tend to be small (with some notable exceptions), and multinationality is a feature of some important industries.

NOTES

1. This matrix draws upon the methods and experience gained from constructing similar matrices for the manufacturing sector of the EU for the years 1987 (Davies and Lyons et al., 1996) and 1993 (Davies, Rondi and Sembenelli, 1998).
2. In fact, the matrix probably also includes most of the top 30 firms – the only probable top 30 firms not on the matrix are Cora, Comptoirs Modernes and Kwik Save.
3. This appears to be for two reasons. First, as mentioned earlier, many previous estimates have been based on measures of market size which are too low, and this means concentration will have been over-estimated. Second, some previous estimates have included buying groups as single entities, and this obviously increases the share of the top 5 'firms'. For example, this is presumably the reason why one source cites CR5 for Italy as high as 58.5 per cent. The other major feature of this table is the surprisingly wide variance in estimates among previous estimates for the same country. For example, CR5 in Italy varies between 21 per cent and 59 per cent, in Germany between 37 per cent and 74 per cent, and so on. This underlines the need for a set of estimates which have been constructed on an internally consistent basis. Hopefully our estimates have achieved that objective.
4. The data relate to 1996 and do not take account of the more recent growth of Tesco which has increased its market share to about 22 per cent (while the share of Sainsbury remains largely unchanged).
5. More recently, in 1999, Wal-Mart has acquired Asda (the fourth ranked UK firm).
6. In accounting terms, cross border activity is the third part of a relationship which links concentration at the EU level to concentration within individual member states.
7. In fact, in 1993 and 1996, just Denmark.
8. Of course, CR5 is also adjusted by subtracting the share of any firms displaced from the top 5, or who belong to the buying group now included.
9. It should be noted, therefore, that the firms are not ranked in order of the *absolute* magnitudes of their foreign activity: this is why, say, Spar Osterreich and Dansk Supermarkt feature so high in the list – they are relatively small firms, but with a large proportion of their turnover outside their home bases.

PART III: CASE STUDIES

In this part of the book we present detailed case studies designed to examine the experience of different countries and specific products at a disaggregated level. In particular, we focus on market structure in the different countries and its relationship to buying power and the possible existence of anti-competitive practices. In discussing the cases, we also provide necessary background on the countries/products as a basis for comparative analysis.

In what follows, we focus on four countries: France, Germany, Spain and the UK, and three specific products: washing powders and detergents, coffee, and butter and margarine. These were selected in part because we had access to experts in these countries who were able to provide us with country-specific information on the food retail distribution sector, but, more importantly, because they represent a good cross-section of the different experience of countries in the EU. Thus, the UK has relatively high concentration in food retailing, and has the largest share of own brand sales; Germany is distinguished by its discount chains, which have induced fierce competition at the retail stage; in France, there has been considerable growth in hypermarket groups which have also sought to expand into other countries in the EU; and in Spain, concentration is lower, although more recently it has been increasing at a rapid rate.

Although there are differences between the countries, it is important to note that there are strong similarities too. In all countries concentration in food retailing is increasing, and likely to increase further in the years ahead. In many markets, this has led to bilateral oligopoly situations arising where retailer chains and major European producers individually engage in bilateral negotiations over prices, fees paid, product positioning and so on. Nevertheless, a common concern of suppliers is that retailer chains have 'excessive' buying power which allows them to 'squeeze' low prices out of dependent suppliers and obtain unjustified fees and rebates and dictate other contractual obligations such as exclusive supply obligations.

In undertaking these studies, we made use of published information such as company reports, trade journals, published work and so on. In addition, our researchers used questionnaires and interviews with producers, retailer chains, buying groups and others (e.g. retail associations, producer organisations, competition authorities and Government agencies) to supplement the desk study work. In all, there were interviews (or questionnaires returned) from 47 individuals or organisations, including 24 suppliers, nine retailers, three buying groups and 11 others (see the appendix for details.) These interviews and

99

responses yielded valuable insights and provided a firmer understanding of the issues at stake in each particular case.

We report the results of our investigations for each of the countries in Chapters 8–11, with details on the three specific product categories at the end of each country case. A summary of the lessons arising from the cases is contained in Chapter 12.

8. Food Retailing in France

8.1 MARKET STRUCTURE CHARACTERISTICS AND EVOLUTION

France has a dense retail network of both traditional and modern stores, even if traditional food retailing is declining. Since 1970, the food retailing market share of supermarkets and hypermarkets in France has quadrupled, to the detriment of small independent stores. More than 60 per cent of French consumers' food purchases are now made in supermarkets or hypermarkets, as shown in Table 8.1.

Table 8.1 Market share by type of outlet (% sales)

Type of Outlet	1970	1980	1997
Hypermarkets (>2,500m²)	3.6	14.3	33.0
Supermarkets (between 400 and 2,500 m²)	9.0	16.8	28.3
Other big shops	20.7	13.7	1.5
Small shops, including specialists	66.7	55.2	37.2

Source: INSEE, 1988.

In 1998, according to INSEE, 36 per cent of French households shopped in two different stores, 29 per cent shopped in only one store, 16 per cent shopped in three stores, and 15 per cent never went to a supermarket at all. Consumers also choose their main store principally according to practical criteria (67 per cent of consumers choose one of their closest stores). Price is the main criterion for only 16 per cent of households, choice for 11 per cent and quality for five per cent. But when two stores are equidistant from their household, they tend to choose the cheapest: hypermarket and supermarket chains in France are involved in a very intense price competition. Delivering the lowest price is the aim of most of these chains.

Table 8.2 shows total sales in France in FFr. billion of the leading hypermarket and supermarket chains in 1996 and 1997. Intermarché is the largest group with sales of FFr. 142 billion although Carrefour, if one includes

Table 8.2   Grocery sales in France (FFr. bn), 1996–97

Groups	1996	1997
Intermarché (TTC)	139.6	141.7
Carrefour	92.2	96.2
Leclerc (TTC)	136.0	140.0
Auchan	n.a.	79.0
Promodès	66.5	67.5
Casino	58.3	67.0
Système U (TTC)	43.0	50.6
Cora (41% owned by Carrefour)	34.0	34.0
Comptoirs Modernes	28.2	30.5

Note: TTC means taxes included.

Source: COB, 1998.

sales of Comptoirs Modernes[1] and Cora, is close behind. Leclerc also has sales
of FFr. 140 billion, with other groups some way behind. Table 8.3 shows global
sales of the main groups where Carrefour, if one includes Comptoirs Modernes

Table 8.3   Total grocery sales for each group (FFr. bn), 1992–97

Groups	1992	1993	1994	1995	1996	1997
Intermarché	113.6	n.a.	109.0	116.0	139.6	195.0
Carrefour	117.1	124.5	136.3	144.6	154.9	169.3
Leclerc	113.8	n.a.	112.5	117.0	136.0	140.0
Auchan	85.1	n.a.	60.6	64.3	120.0	130.0
Promodès[a]	84.2	90.2	94.7	100.6	103.5	110.0
Casino	61.6	63.1	63.0	64.1	66.8	74.5
Docks de France[b]	32.0	n.a.	43.5	46.7	-	-
Système U	40.0	n.a.	n.a.	n.a.	43.0	50.5
Cora	n.a.	n.a.	n.a.	n.a.	39.0[c]	46.0
Comptoirs Modernes	22.6	23.6	25.7	27.0	30.2	32.1

Notes:
a. Promodès turnover is about FFr. 170 billion in 1997 when including franchisee sales.
b. Taken over by Auchan in 1996.
c. FFr. 45 billion when including the Belgian group Louis Delhaize, 41 per cent owned by Cora and
    managed by Cora.

Source: COB, 1998.

and Cora, is the leading group, and Intermarché is in second place. These two chains are by far the largest in these terms and foreign sales are important, in particular, for Carrefour, Promodès and Auchan.

Hypermarkets dominate the French retailing system: they are responsible for 47 per cent of general food retailing (excluding specialised food stores such as bakers or butchers shops). Supermarkets on this measure account for 37 per cent of sales, discounters four per cent and general grocery stores 12 per cent. Food sales account for about 55 per cent of sales of hypermarkets, and 80 per cent of supermarket sales.

Table 8.4 shows the leading hypermarket groups. Leclerc is by far the largest, followed by Carrefour, Géant and Mammouth. Table 8.5 shows the evolution of the largest supermarket groups. Here Intermarché stands out as the largest group, followed, at a distance, by Champion and Super U.

Table 8.4 Evolution of the number of hypermarkets for each group

Group	1988	1992	1996
Leclerc	155	298	373
Carrefour	68	109	117
Géant (Casino)	24	49	108
Mammouth (Paridoc)	76	86	92
Continente (Promodès)	34	65	84
Cora	46	49	54
Auchan	39	49	52
Hyper U	-	18	33
Hyper Champion	-	-	12
Total number of hypermarkets	725	950	1060

Note: These statistics do not take account of the average sales area of each store: in 1996, Carrefour owned fewer hypermarkets than Leclerc, but the two groups had the same total sales area.

Source: Linéaires, 1998.

The French retailing industry has become increasingly concentrated in the last ten years. According to AC Nielsen, in 1997 the five main retailers shared 67.2 per cent of the market, whereas they shared only 55.7 per cent in 1992. Our own estimates (from Chapter 7)[2] show lower levels of concentration, but still a notable increase from 48 per cent to 51 per cent in 1993–96 (Table 8.6). Clearly, at these lower levels, concentration is significant and increasing. In this table, Intermarché and Promodès are the leading groups, although, as before, Carrefour is the largest if Auchan and Comptoirs Modernes are included with it. Leclerc has lost market share while that of Auchan has increased.

Table 8.5 Evolution of the number of supermarkets for each group

Group	1988	1992	1996
Intermarché	1,114	1,613	1,646
Champion	232	467	536
Super U	250	498	513
Casino	n.a.	259	380
Stoc	199	326	369
Atac	n.a.	205	326
Monoprix	126	n.a.	198
Prisunic	207	187	181
Match	n.a.	156	164
Leclerc	335	227	136
Total number of supermarkets	6070	7412	7670

Source: Linéaires, 1998.

Table 8.6 Market shares, 1993 and 1997

Group	1993 (%)	1996 (%)
Intermarché	11.6	11.9
Promodès	9.3	10.1
Leclerc	12.2	9.7
Carrefour	8.4	9.7
Auchan	5.7	9.4
Casino	6.0	6.3
CR5	47.5	50.8

Source: Authors'estimates (see Chapter 7).

A number of significant mergers have taken place, and this has facilitated the growth in market shares of the firms involved. The first important merger in recent years happened in 1991 when Carrefour acquired Euromarché for FFr. 5.5 bn (Euromarché's turnover was about FFr. 27 bn at the time). In 1992, Casino took over Rallye (whose turnover was about FFr. 20 bn). Auchan became the fifth national group in 1996 thanks to its acquisition of Docks de France. Promodès tried to increase its size in 1997 by announcing a take-over bid for Casino, but the board of Casino refused the offer and Promodès failed in its attempt. Finally, the recent acquisition of Comptoirs Modernes by Carrefour (who already owned part of the firm) in 1998 allowed this hypermarket-specialised group to diversify its retailing network into supermarkets, and to recover its leading position.

Independent groups have also sought to increase their size: Leclerc and Système U concluded a co-operation agreement in 1998. Both groups retain their own names, but they intend to negotiate their supplies together. If they were to merge, they would be the largest retailing group in France.

Several factors have fostered merger activity, among them the progressive saturation of the French market and the slow growth of household consumption, which has restrained the growth in turnover of leading retailing chains.

During the last ten years, numerous small retailing groups have disappeared: either being acquired by larger groups or going into liquidation. Among the 50 main supermarket chains in 1986, 21 no longer existed by 1996 and it is estimated that ten others could disappear soon. This evolution is even more remarkable for hypermarkets: 30 different hypermarket names existed in 1986, with only ten remaining by 1998.

Finally, it is worth noting the recent development of deep discounters in France. The first deep discount stores were opened in 1988 by the German groups Lidl and Aldi. They are still not very developed, partly because of the discount pricing of the main groups, but their turnover is increasing. In 1991, hard discount stores (mainly supermarkets) provided only 1.3 per cent of food sales in French self-service stores. In 1996, they accounted for 7.5 per cent of food sales. The leading hard-discount chains are German: Lidl is the market leader, but French groups have responded more recently by creating their own hard discount subsidiaries. For example, Carrefour created Ed which is now the second largest hard discounter in France. Casino bought 70 per cent of Baud-Franprix and now owns the fourth largest hard-discount chain with its 265 Leader Price outlets.

Consumers seem to have benefited from the development of mass distribution, and, in particular, from the strong price competition it has induced. In the 1980s the government considered the development of mass distribution as an instrument to fight against inflation. On the other hand, consumers sometimes complain about the decreasing number of small independent stores, and they accuse the big retailing chains of squeezing out small shopkeepers. This was an argument for the Galland law (see below). But on the whole, the first effect seems to override the second, and consumers have benefited from the development of mass retailers where there have been significant efficiency improvements.

The leading French retailing chains agree that the wave of great mergers and take-overs will go on over the coming years, especially among French groups. Even the independent groups have started a rapprochement, as shown by the co-operation agreement signed by Leclerc and Système U in 1998. Moreover, the Conseil de la Concurrence (the Competition Council) does not seem disposed to prevent new mergers, as shown for example in its 1997 report.

Other legislative developments have, however, been used. Introduced in 1996, the Raffarin law[3] regulates the opening of new stores with a sales area over 300 m². Each project has to be accepted by a regional commission and these commissions are also able to prevent the extension of current premises. Furthermore, in 1996, the government decided to stop all extensions during a six month period. In 1997, 25 per cent of new stores were rejected by the commissions, and since 1996 the number of supermarkets opening has decreased significantly (less than two hundred per year since 1996, while there were more than three hundred per year between 1986 and 1995).

The retail network in France is quite dense and is nearly saturated. Because of this the leading retailing groups (especially Intermarché and Carrefour) increasingly focus on expansion abroad, and they scarcely attempt to open new outlets in France. In 1996, only 24 hypermarkets were opened, among which 19 were in fact upgrades from supermarkets to hypermarkets. About 70 per cent of the supermarkets that opened in 1996 were deep discount stores, mostly belonging to foreign groups. The recent development of these kinds of outlets, whose names were previously unknown, shows that there are few barriers to entry for retailers providing new kinds of services, like deep discount. But there certainly are more significant barriers to entry in classical food retailing in France, as it would be very difficult for an unknown retailer to succeed in opening a hypermarket in France.

Besides the Raffarin law, the 1996 Galland law[4] has had an important impact on the relationships between manufacturers and retailers in France. This law has two purposes. First, the government wanted to reduce the imbalance between suppliers and retailers by limiting the buying power of retail chains. The second aim was to protect small shopkeepers from the competition of large retail chains. The Galland law brought six main changes in French regulation:

- invoicing rules were changed, such that rebates now have to appear on bills and cannot be negotiated at the end of the year. Furthermore, commercial services offered by retailers (e.g. end-of-aisle displays or promotional activities) have to be put on a special bill rather than being negotiated ad hoc.
- selling at a loss is now completely forbidden, and the threshold is now defined by the price charged on the bill (with the new invoicing rules) plus transportation costs and taxes. Retailers can no longer set retail prices below wholesale prices for loss leaders and recover a profit by charging the producers for services or asking for a rebate.
- 'excessively low prices' are forbidden. This rule completes the ban on selling at a loss, and is aimed primarily at own brands. 'Excessively low prices' are not defined exactly in the law, but the intention is to include low prices compared to costs of production and distribution.

- refusal to supply is now permitted.
- listing fees without any real benefits (i.e. services provided by the retailer) are not permitted. Furthermore, retailers asking for a listing fee have now to commit to a minimum amount of purchase, which has to be in proportion to the fee. (The law does not mention what proportion should be used).
- finally, a retailer who wishes to stop purchasing a particular product has to give prior written notice to the producer and vice versa.

At present the law has had mixed effects. In part, this is due to the ambiguity of the wording, as, for example, in the case of listing fees. In addition, the right of producers to refuse to supply certain retail outlets can be seen as anti- rather than pro-competitive. This provision, in support of producers, allows them to choose their own retailing network and, for example, will allow producers of household appliances not to supply discount stores. This provision, however, does not affect food retailing.

The law has had an impact on retail prices: according to Nielsen, the prices of well-known brands sold by hypermarkets increased by more than four per cent during the first half of 1997. This effect was softened a few months later, and after an adaptation period, prices fell slightly. Also the number of products sold at a loss seems to have decreased dramatically. The Galland law has had an effect on the development of own brands (further details are given in Section 8.4). Moreover, the prohibition on selling at a loss has enhanced the pressure exerted by retailers on producers to reduce their prices.

8.2 RETAILER BUYING POWER

The recent wave of mergers in French retailing is likely to have increased retailer buying power, even if producers are quite concentrated in some markets. Carrefour or Intermarché, for instance, with a turnover of about FFr. 150 bn, appear to have a stronger position, say, than the leading French food producer, Danone, with its FFr. 88bn turnover. Moreover, large retail chains' market valuation is increasing rapidly. Between 1995 and 1997, the market capitalisation of the three main listed retail chains (Carrefour, Promodès and

Table 8.7 Changes in market capitalisation, 1995–97

CAC 40	Carrefour	Promodès	Casino
+ 62%	+179%	+144%	+90%

Source: Linéaires, 1998.

Casino) increased by more than the CAC 40 (Table 8.7). This, of course, partly reflects take-over activity, particularly by Carrefour.

The main retail chains account for a significant part of many producers' sales. For example, Table 8.8 shows the share of Intermarché in the sales of some food brands in 1991. These proportions indicate that producers (especially small producers), depend heavily on Intermarché for their sales, and this means that they could be at a bargaining disadvantage in selling to this chain. While this may not always be the case, especially where large producers are concerned, it indicates that buying power of large retail groups may well exist.

Table 8.8 Intermarché's buying market share for several food brands, 1991

Belin (biscuits)	15 %	Poulain (chocolate)	20 %
Maxwell (coffee)	18 %	Panzani (pasta)	18 %
Vittel (water)	16 %	Lesieur (oils and fats)	18 %

Source: Interviews.

Bulk buying undoubtedly generates reduced costs, but discounts obtained by the major retail chains appear to result largely from their buying power. For instance, Danone's operating income decreased from ten per cent to 8.8 per cent between 1992 and 1995, whereas Carrefour's gross profit increased from 16.8 per cent to 18.5 per cent during the same period and this may indicate (albeit in fairly crude terms) the shifting of power between producers and retail groups. Retailer average gross margins for different products are shown in Table 8.9.

Table 8.9 Retailer average gross margins by product category, 1994

Fresh products	Grocery	Drinks	Frozen items	Average (food)
15 %	16 %	15 %	17 %	14.5 %

Source: GEA.

Our interviews suggest that retailers refuse to purchase leading brands fairly infrequently but they might threaten to do so when they negotiate with producers. Small producers face more difficulties in dealing with big retail chains: whereas retailers claim to develop 'partnerships' with small firms. But these small producers do not seem completely satisfied, as a recent study by ETHIC[5] shows. Small producers had to identify the two main factors of dysfunction in their relationships with retailers. Table 8.10 shows the results. Clearly, the suggestion that negotiators change too frequently, selected in over

60 per cent of responses, suggests that the relationships between producers and retailers are not likely to be that close.

Table 8.10 Small producer problems with large retailers

The negotiators change too frequently	60.2 %
The terms of agreements are not respected	43.3 %
The agreements are constantly modified	37.8 %
There are too many negotiators	28.9 %
Retailing structures are not clear	26.4 %

Source: ETHIC, 1998.

Recent cases of refusal to purchase in the mineral water market indicate that retailers sometimes prefer to lose turnover by de-listing major brands. Such action is useful in illustrating that a threat is credible, even if it induces losses in the short run. The Competition Authority in France has considered several cases of refusal to purchase recently, in several different markets.

Small suppliers are usually unable to impose conditions on major retail chains. Retailing conditions are, of course, discussed, but discussions are usually linked to services provided and charged for by retailers. Large producers seem to be able to resist pressure from the major chains, as observed by the Conseil de la Concurrence in its 1994 report on the washing powders market (see section 8.6.1 below).

8.3 BUYING GROUPS

There are several different kinds of buying groups in France. First, integrated buying groups (owned by one firm) are the oldest. In most cases, smaller groups have joined these integrated buying groups. For instance Cap, the Promodès food buying group, has independent affiliated firms, like Prisunic, which was part of Pinault-Printemps and was bought out by Monoprix in October 1997. Smaller buying groups sometimes join larger ones: thus Francap which combines independent wholesalers working for small stores (its turnover is about FFr. 18 bn) joined Casino's buying group in 1996.

Second, some buying groups are owned by several firms, like Francap or Paridoc. Finally there are independent buying groups, like Leclerc, Système U and Intermarché, who often have their own national and regional supplying system. Usually, producers have to negotiate first with the national buying group that lists their products without quantity pre-commitment. Then they also have to negotiate at a regional level and finally perhaps with each store. This process seems more complicated for producers than direct negotiation with a national buying group.

In the mid-1980s, some 'super-buying groups' were created, sometimes uniting very different distributors with diverging goals. Thus buying groups like Alci, Difra or Socadip appeared but most of them collapsed soon after because of the diversity of their members. Moreover, the concentration wave in French

Table 8.11 Main buying groups and their members, 1996

Buying Group	Market share in food retailing	
Cometca	17.9	
Carrefour + Ed		13.1
Comptoirs Modernes		3.0
Métro France		1.8
Leclerc (GALEC)	15.3	
Intermarché	15.1	
Paridoc	14.1	
Groupe Auchan		12.4
Coop Atlantique		0.6
Guyenne & Gascogne, PG, Chareton, Schiever		1.1
CAP	12.7	
Promodès		11.0
Prisunic		0.7
Hyparlo, Provencia		1.0
Casino	12.3	
Groupe Casino		7.5
Monoprix		2.1
Coop. de Normandie		0.5
Francap Alimentaire		1.2
Système U	1.2	
Locéda	5.7	
Groupe Cora		4.3
Catteau-Tesco France		0.6
Coop d'Alsace		0.4
La Moderne, Migros		0.4

Source: AC Nielsen/Linéaires, 1996.

food retailing appears instrumental in the decline of some super-buying groups. When Carrefour, which had its own buying group, bought Euromarché in 1991, Socadip could not survive the 30 billion francs loss due to Euromarché's departure. Now most of the buying groups are composed of a dominant large retailer joined by small satellite retailers (Table 8.11).

Large buying groups typically refuse members with too low a turnover. However, it is possible for small retailers to join small buying groups which can join larger ones. Thus, Francap members, for example, are now affiliated to Casino's buying group.

At present, retail buying groups at the European level exist but these appear to have had limited success as far as retail buying is concerned in France. An example is Leclerc which joined the EMD (European Marketing Distribution) group in 1997. The main reason for the lack of impact so far appears to be the divergence of interests of the members of these groups. This recalls the lack of co-ordination in the 'super-buying groups'. At present, European-based buying groups appear mainly to be operating in low-price items often sold by discounters.

8.4 OWN BRANDS

While not having developed as far as in the UK, own brands are of growing importance in France. This is due, in part, to the retailers' ability to extract lower purchase prices from suppliers of own brands which enables them to set higher margins. In addition, with the passing of the Galland law, retailers have a stronger incentive to sell their own brands since provisions in the law have strengthened the hand of branded good producers. According to an inquiry conducted by INSEE in April 1998, 72 per cent of customers who regularly frequent supermarkets or hypermarkets buy own brands. Also, 13 per cent ignore own brands entirely even though own brands are already in most stores. However, consumers still often confuse own brands and low price products. Over the past few years, retailers have been seeking to increase own brand quality, and they now try to create innovative products under their own names to enhance their reputation. As a result, own brands have increased the competition between producers for shelf space in supermarkets. Table 8.12 gives own brand market shares for the main retailers in 1996.

Table 8.13 illustrates the development of own brand market shares in supermarkets and hypermarkets. Own brand growth is an important trend in the recent evolution of distribution. In 1995, own brands provided on average 20 per cent of sales (25 per cent of shelf space) compared to about ten per cent ten years before, and the development goes on. Leclerc, for instance, which was initially opposed to own brand development (less than seven per cent of sales before 1997 were own brand), changed its strategy in 1997 and its goal is now to double its own brands' turnover. Retailers try to reinforce the association between their name and their own products.

Table 8.12 Own brand shares (food only) for leading retailers, 1996

Names	Own brands' market share	Number of items
Franprix	28.0	n.a.
Casino	24.8	1800
Intermarché	24.7	2500
Géant	20.0	1800
Carrefour	18.9	1642
Monoprix	18.7	1800
Système U	18.5	985
Continente	17.8	1440
Stoc	16.2	650
Auchan	15.7	1500
Match	15.4	1100
Champion	15.1	1240
Leclerc	14.8	500
Cora	12.2	1224
Prisunic	11.7	550

Source: Secodip-linéaires, 1997.

Table 8.13 National brand, own brand and low price item shares for supermarkets and hypermarkets (%)

	1991	1994	1995	1996
National brands	80.6	75.0	75.3	76.0
Own brands	14.7	17.1	17.4	17.1
Low price items	4.7	7.9	7.3	6.9

Source: LSA, 1998.

Table 8.14 gives own brands' market shares for the main retailers in 1993. As noted above, retailers set higher margins on own brands than on other brands even if retail prices are lower. According to ICC 95, the mark-up rate fixed by retailers is estimated on average at 23 per cent of the turnover for own brands, 15 per cent for low price products and 14.5 per cent for national brands. Moreover, shelf space profitability is higher: if the gross mark-up per square meter of shelf space index is 100 then own brands' profitability is 123, low price items' profitability is 63 and national brands' profitability is 103.

Table 8.14 Own brand shares for leading retailers, 1993

Retailer	Own Brand Market Shares
Monoprix	28%
Casino	25%
Intermarché	23%
Carrefour	22%
Auchan	19%
Leclerc	10%

Source: GIRA, 1993–94.

8.5 INTERNATIONALISATION

Internationalisation has been an important feature of French hypermarket and supermarket chains. There are two main reasons why such internationalisation exists. First, the French food retail market is fairly saturated, and, in particular with the Raffarin law recently introduced, future hypermarket or supermarket growth within France is more difficult. Second, international subsidiaries tend to be more profitable than domestic ones, particularly in countries in southern (or eastern) Europe where large store development lags behind. In fact, French companies began moving into other countries in the early 1970s and this process has continued ever since.

Table 8.15 shows foreign turnover by the leading retail groups in 1997. Much of the expansion has been undertaken by Carrefour (which also acquired Comptoirs Modernes in 1997), Promodès and Auchan. Carrefour, for example, opened its first hypermarket 'Pryca' in Spain in 1973 (in Barcelona) and now has 56 'Pryca' stores. Promodès moved into Spain in 1976 and now has 52 hypermarkets 'Continente', 1,830 discount stores 'Dia' and 33 cash and carrys 'Puntocash'. Non-integrated groups such as Leclerc have been slower to start international development, although Leclerc now has 11 stores abroad. Intermarché recently bought 75 per cent of Spar, the fifth largest German distribution group.

Greece and Italy offer real growth prospects to the extent that a strict legislative system has delayed retail trade evolution for a long time. East European countries also offer new outlets for the largest French groups. In particular, Poland is an emerging market with an underdeveloped market structure and growing consumers' buying power. Casino, Auchan and also some non-integrated groups have already begun to locate stores in Poland. As this trend continues, companies such as Carrefour and Promodès will look increasingly to buying supplies on a European level, and this will heighten the buying power of such groups.

Table 8.15 Foreign turnover of leading French retail groups, 1997

Groups	Foreign turnover (FFr. bn)	% of Total Turnover
Carrefour	62.7	40.5
Promodès	37.0	35.7
Auchan	23.5	19.5
Cora	11.0	24.0
Casino	8.5	11.5
Comptoirs Modernes	2.0	7.0

Source: Linéaires, Interviews.

8.6 PRODUCTS

8.6.1 Washing Powders and Detergents

The market for washing products in France represents 60 per cent of the total detergents market. It is quite strongly segmented, as each brand exists in several formats (standard powder, liquid, concentrated, and, recently, tablets) and in various container sizes. This segmentation is a central issue in the negotiations between producers and retailers: producers develop innovations to bring about market growth, and they create a number of new reference points, whereas retailers face increasing difficulties in handling this product proliferation and the ensuing complexity of the range of products. More particularly, the launching of compact powders initially suited both producers and retailers because of the potential growth it offered and because of the decrease in logistical costs it was supposed to bring. Yet it did not seem to suit consumers, since nearly 50 per cent of them now still buy standard powder, as shown in Table 8.16. The number of reference points listed by retailers has thus increased: there are about 130 reference points in the average hypermarket, and about 85 in the average supermarket.

The market for washing powders is dominated by four international groups, which compete at a European and a world-wide level. The market is very concentrated, since these four companies produce 94 per cent of sales, while the rest is now almost completely composed of own brands.

Table 8.16 Market segmentation in washing powders (%)

Market segment	1991	1997
Standard	47	49.3
Liquid	20	13.8
Concentrated liquid	-	9.9
Concentrated	24	16.9
Special	9	10.1

Source: LSA, 1998.

Table 8.17 Market shares of leading producers of washing powders (%)

Producers	Main Brands	Market shares: 1988	1990	1995	1996	1997
Procter & Gamble	Ariel, Vizir, Bonux	34.5	35.5	36.7	38.2	37.6
Lever	Skip, Omo, Persil	28.0	27.0	23.3	22.5	22.9
Henkel	Le Chat, Super Croix	20.0	18.5	21.4	20.6	21.3
Colgate Palmolive	Dash, Axion, Gama	11.5	11.0	12.3	12.8	12.2
Own brands		6.0	8.0	6.3	5.9	6.0

Note: For 1988 and 1990, own brands includes 'others' and 'own brands'.

Source: LSA, 1998.

Market shares have been quite stable for the last ten years with P&G the market leader with 38 per cent of sales in 1997, followed by Lever (23 per cent), Henkel (21 per cent) and Colgate Palmolive (12 per cent) (Table 8.17). Own brands' market share increased at the end of the eighties, but since then they have not increased, and their market share has even decreased slightly. Also at the end of the nineties, small independent brands have disappeared from the shelves. The main reason for this appears to have been the high level of advertising of branded goods, and the strong brand allegiance that this creates. In addition, the major producers produce brands for each segment of the market (Table 8.18) and this makes it difficult for new firms/products to find a niche in which to make a profit. Also, recently introduced washing tablets are well protected by patents, and this makes it difficult for other firms (e.g. producing own brands) to produce their own versions of this product.

Table 8.18 Leading brands by market segment

	Up-market	Medium	Down-market
Procter & Gamble	Ariel	Vizir	Bonux
Lever	Skip	Omo	Persil
Henkel	Le Chat	Super Croix	-
Colgate Palmolive	Dash	Axion	Gama

Source: LSA, 1998.

Negotiations between producers and retailers in this market focus on a number of factors such as rebates, listing fees, services to be provided by retailers, slotting allowances and so on. Given the limited number of groups on both sides of the market, terms and conditions are normally established by secret bilateral negotiation which can also lead to discriminatory financial conditions between retailers. The market has also been apparently affected by de-listing of products, and, in some cases, refusal to supply.

In 1994, the Conseil de la Concurrence carried out an investigation[6] into the market for washing powders in France. This inquiry revealed the existence of a number of anti-competitive practices, mainly concerning the relationship between manufacturers and retailers.

Among other things, the Conseil found:

- a number of more or less hidden rebates and fees paid by producers to hypermarket or supermarket groups. These payments were part of confidential agreements (i.e. not written into official prices) but were often included in 'commercial co-operation budgets', 'advertising budgets' and so on. The Conseil identified eight separate types of payment, and criticised the producers for special payments made to Intermarché, GALEC (the buying group for Leclerc) and Système U, along with criticising the retailers for undertaking these arrangements.
- several cases of de-listing had occurred. For example, in 1989, Sachap (the regional buying group for Leclerc) refused to purchase Lever's brands, in protest against Intermarché's low prices, which, according to Sachap, revealed discriminatory conditions. Lever's brands were boycotted for four months, until Lever paid a special fee.
- producers often try to impose conditions on retailers and sometimes use practices like resale price maintenance or refusal to deal. For instance, Henkel was criticised for having imposed a minimum retail price on its

main retailers. Moreover, these minimum prices were found to be discriminatory. At the same time, Procter & Gamble proposed recommended prices and was not criticised. Also, the four main producers refused to supply some products to Intermarché in 1989 and 1990 in protest against the retailer selling at a loss.

- finally, there was some evidence that branded washing powders were sold at a loss. Competition on branded washing powders is very intense at the retail level, and margins are typically very thin and, in some cases, negative. In 1994, for example, Lever accused Intermarché of selling its brands at a loss when Intermarché published a promotion catalogue which announced a retail price for Lever's brands that undercut the wholesale price by 2.5 per cent.

We spoke to several leading producers in this market. They argued that buying power was a very important problem in France. Yet it appears that the brand leaders have very strong brands and this strengthens their bargaining power with retailers. Refusal to purchase is now relatively rare and it seems unlikely that own brands will increase market share markedly from the level so far attained. On the other hand, one major concern of retailers is to limit the increasing number of reference points, and to avoid over-segmentation of the market. They are trying to obtain the removal of some products from the market and this is an on-going issue between retailers and producers.

8.6.2 Coffee

The coffee market has two main sub-markets: roast and ground coffee and instant coffee. In France, instant coffee constitutes 20 per cent of total coffee consumption by volume compared to nearly 90 per cent (by sales value) in the UK. In the roast and ground coffee market there are three main segments: Arabica, mixed coffee and decaffeinated coffee, but a narrower market segmentation would also distinguish different quality levels.

Table 8.19 shows the evolution of the share of the average consumer's budget allocated to the consumption of coffee (and other beverages). After a fall at the beginning of the nineties, the share of the consumer's budget allocated to the consumption of coffee (and other beverages) has increased again, and its level in 1996 is slightly higher than in 1990. However, tea and other beverage consumption has increased in this period, and, in fact, coffee consumption declined slightly in 1996 (and 1997).

One of the main reasons for this is the rise of the world price of Arabica (+ 50 per cent) and of Robusta (+ 40 per cent) in 1997. This increase affected prices in supermarkets by 25 per cent to 40 per cent. Distributors reflect the increase in these costs in national brands of coffee although to some extent they smooth out price increases for own brands and low price coffee.

Table 8.19 Coffee (and other beverages) in the average consumer budget

Years	1990	1992	1993	1994	1995	1996
Budget Coefficient for Coffee, Tea, Herb Tea	0.323	0.272	0.265	0.290	0.340	0.346

Source: INSEE 1995, 1996.

Table 8.20 shows the sales of roast and instant coffee in France for 1998.

Table 8.20 Sales of coffee in France, 1998

Product	Roast coffee	Instant Coffee
Turnover in FFr. Millions	7581	2517

Source: EUROSTAT, 1998.

The two main producers of roast coffee in France are Kraft Jacobs Suchard which has a market share of 44 per cent and Douwe Egberts' with a market share of about 16 per cent (Table 8.21). Italian groups like Lavazza and Segafredo and the French group Legal follow. Own brand market share is growing with sales of 17 per cent in 1997. The market for instant coffee, which is, of course, much smaller, is dominated by Nestlé with Nescafé having nearly 70 per cent of the market. The second producer in the French market is Maxwell, a General Foods subsidiary, whose market share is about 15 per cent. Own brands provide 6.2 per cent of the market and other brands 8.8 per cent.

The major producers of coffee are subject to pressure from the major retailing chains to reduce prices for this product. In particular, when the coffee price increases (as for instance occurred during the summer of 1994 and at the end of 1996), retailers may try to impose a delay on producers before they can pass the increase on in wholesale prices. This delay enables retailers to lay in stocks, and when producers raise their prices retailers need to purchase less coffee. This can explain, at least in part, why retail prices do not always reflect changes in the underlying coffee price. As the coffee price is very volatile, producers tend to bear a larger part of costs induced by market volatility.

In this market, retail prices usually reflect wholesale prices, as retailers typically charge a very small mark-up for the major coffee brands, because coffee has traditionally been considered a loss leader or very low-margin item. Nevertheless, since the Galland law forbids sales at a loss, retailers are no longer able to have negative margins. As with other products (and other countries) retailers charge higher margins on own brand products.

Table 8.21 Leading brand market shares, 1996 and 1997 (%)

Brands	Market shares by volume (1996)	Market shares by volume (1997)
Maison du Café (Douwe Egberts)	14.9	16.5
Carte Noire (KJS)	17.0	16.5
Jacques Vabre (KJS)	14.2	13.8
Grand Mère (KJS)	13.2	13.2
Lavazza	7.0	6.2
Segafredo	5.8	5.4
Legal	5.6	4.5
Malongo	3.0	3.1
Own Brands and First Price Products	15.9	17.3
Other Brands	3.3	3.4

Source: LSA Février, 1998.

Coffee is similar to other products in that retail grocery chains often ask coffee producers to pay for special services. These services are, for instance, communication services (regional advertisements) or fees for end-of-aisle displays, that tend to increase the demand for a brand. This allows retailers to obtain rebates, the amount of which producers estimate at between 15 per cent and 30 per cent of sales. Buying groups can also require up-front fees from the producers.

Refusal to purchase appears rare in this market, but sometimes a retailer may stop listing one brand which for a secondary producer can induce serious losses.

It is expected in the next few years that concentration in the roast coffee market will increase, although own brands will also probably increase their market share. As in other markets this will put pressure on secondary producers. In this case, however, the low technology involved and the availability of sales to restaurants and cafés (accounting for 30 per cent of total consumption) mean that a sizeable number of secondary producers are likely to survive. In the instant sector, Nestlé is likely to continue to dominate the market.

8.6.3 Butter and Margarine

The butter and non-butter spreads market is divided into three segments in France: butter, margarine and low fat products (typically with less than a 60 per cent fat content). Sales of butter (the largest segment) were FFr. 6.0 billion in

1997 (Table 8.22) compared to margarine (FFr. 1.4 billion) and low fats (FFr. 0.8 billion). Consumption of margarine is much lower in France than the European average, with 3.5 kg/hab/year in 1997 compared to 6kg/hab/year.

Table 8.22 Total turnover of butter and margarine, 1997

Products	Butter	Margarine	Low fat products
Turnover FFr. mn	6028	1385	836

Source: EUROSTAT, 1998.

In the butter sector, the market is very atomistic and own brands and low price products represent more than two thirds of the market by volume. The four leading brands, Président, Elle & Vire, Paysan Breton and Bridel represent only thirty one per cent of the market (Table 8.23).

On the other hand, margarine is dominated by Unilever which controls Astra Calvé and supplies nearly half of the margarine market. In this sub-market, own brands and first price products represent about one third of the market. Vamo is the main company that produces first price products and own brands for supermarkets. To capture consumers, margarine producers adopt two kinds of strategy. The first one concerns the design of products: margarine is sold in small tubs instead of packs. The second strategy consists of a very high segmentation of the market with nearly fifteen brands and only a few producers. In the low fat content sector the leading group Astra Calvé had a 39 per cent market share in 1998 followed by Védial with 35 per cent.

The market for butter is particularly interesting in this case. Given the atomistic nature of supply, retailers are in a strong position to squeeze as much profit as possible out of the small suppliers. Retailers may obtain fees for listing products, for making certain types of shelf space available, for end-of-aisle displays and so on. Moreover, retailers tend to treat butter as a loss leader and often set zero margins on branded butter products, while realising positive margins on own brand products. From the point of view of the consumer, therefore, butter is sold at a very advantageous price. But other, smaller, retailers may suffer as a consequence of this, and producers themselves may be forced to toe the line or lose their sales. There is a case, therefore, for arguing that retailer buying power could be detrimental in this respect i.e. it tends to increase the pressure on small retailers' ability to survive, and similarly small producers.

On the other hand, it could be argued that in terms of economic efficiency, small producers should only be allowed to make normal profits and that pressure by retailers ensures this is so. This ignores the fact, however, that by

Table 8.23 Market shares in butter, margarine and low fat products, 1998

Groups	Butter	Margarine	Low fat products
Astra Calvé	Total: 0%	Total: 47%	Total: 39%
		(Fruit d'or, Plantafin, Equilibre, Effi, Astra, ...)	Fruit d'or (8.4%) Effi (10.5%) Plantafin (20.1%)
Besnier	Total: 18.1%	Total: 0%	Total: 9.5%
	Bfpridel (4.4%) Président (13.5%)		Bridélight (5.6%) Bridélice (3.2%) Président (0.7%)
Cema	-	Primevère (1.3%)	-
CLE	Elles & Vire (6.7%)	-	-
Laïta	Paysan Breton (6.3%)	-	-
Vedial	Total: 0%	Total: 19%	Total: 34.8%
		(Prima, St Hubert 41, Le Fleurier,Mr Tournesol, Tournolive...)	Prima (3.3%) St Hubert 41 (18.7%) Le Fleurier (12.8%)
Own brands	26.9%	19.4%	7%
Others	42.2%	13.3%	9.7%

Source: Iri-Secodip, 19 April 1998 and RIA 1998.

a change of policy, a retailer could effectively put a supplier out of business, and this is clearly a major threat as far as the supplier is concerned.

This raises the issue of economic dependency, and the extent to which retailer power might be a concern for the competition authorities. Our interviews suggest this is a major concern of small suppliers in this market and several agreed to talk to us only on the basis that they would not be named. The typical complaint was that large supermarket chains use their buying power to set uneconomically low prices for suppliers. Similar complaints were also made in other sectors in other countries, notably in Spain and the UK, and these are discussed further in Chapters 10 and 11 respectively.

NOTES

1. Comptoirs Modernes was acquired by Carrefour in 1997.
2. As noted in Chapter 7, our estimates of concentration exclude non-food and related items, and include all food retailing including fast moving consumer goods (fmcg's). This leads to a lower estimate of five firm concentration than usually found in the literature.
3. Loi du 5 Juillet 1996 relative au développement et à la promotion du commerce et de l'artisanat.
4. Loi N. 96-588 du 01 07 1996 sur la loyauté et l'équilibre des relations commerciales.
5. ETHIC is a research group which looks at the relationships between small firms and retailers and was created by the Federation of Trade and Retailing in France.
6. Decision N. 94-D-60, 13th December 1994.

9. German Food Retailing

9.1 MARKET STRUCTURE CHARACTERISTICS AND EVOLUTION

Germany has a somewhat different market structure in food retailing from the other countries we consider. While the German market has developed in similar ways to other countries as far as the reduction in the number of smaller stores and the growth of hypermarkets is concerned, and supermarkets initially gained an increasing market share, recent trends have shown a slight decrease in supermarket share and significant growth by discounters. In particular, since 1992, German discounters have grown to become the leading type of food outlet (after small stores) with nearly 22 per cent of retail food sales in 1997 (Table 9.1). Supermarkets (with less than 1,500 m² of floor space) are now behind them with 20.5 per cent.

Table 9.1 Market share (in turnover) by type of outlet, 1992–97

Type of Outlet	1992	1994	1996	1997
Discounters	17.6	19.9	21.7	21.8
Hypermarkets (>1,500 m²)	16.6	17.5	17.9	18.7
Supermarkets (400–1,500 m²)	21.8	21.4	20.7	20.5
Other big stores	14.1	12.5	11.3	10.9
Small stores, including specialists	29.9	28.7	28.4	28.1

Source: Euromonitor, 1998.

A similar picture is shown in terms of number of outlets. Here, discounters have increased their outlets by 46 per cent in 1992–97 and hypermarkets by 18 per cent. On the other hand, supermarkets have experienced a slight decline, and other big food stores have declined by 8 per cent (Table 9.2).

Germany has experienced low economic growth since reunification and this has led to relatively low growth rates in food prices in nominal terms, and falling prices in real terms. In nominal terms, food prices increased by less than one per cent on average in the years 1992–7. If we allow for inflation, however,

123

they declined by over ten per cent in the period. Against this backdrop, and, in part, also reflecting it in the growth of discounters, price competition in food retailing was very intense in the 1990s.

Table 9.2 Number of food outlets by type, 1992–97

Type of Outlet	1992	1994	1996	1997
Discounters	8388	10073	11580	12220
Hypermarkets (>1,500 m²)	1854	2023	2097	2191
Supermarkets (400–1,500 m²)	9735	9831	9610	9596
Other big stores	48010	43250	40800	39600

Source: Euromonitor, 1998.

In terms of seller concentration, German food retailing is less concentrated than in the UK or France but more concentrated than in Spain. Table 9.3 shows the major food retailing groups in Germany and their estimated market shares in 1993 and 1996. The market leaders are Rewe and Edeka/AVA with market shares of more than ten per cent in 1996. They are followed by Aldi (9 per cent), Metro (8.4 per cent) and Tengelmann (6.7 per cent). Metro is a company group while Edeka and Rewe are co-operatively organised and have some characteristics of a buying group (see below). Aldi is a discounter. There is also

Table 9.3 Market shares (%), 1993 and 1996

Group	1993	1996
Rewe-Group	8.6	10.9
Edeka/AVA-Group	12.2	10.5
Aldi-Group	8.3	9.0
Metro-Group	9.9	8.4
Tengelmann-Group	6.1	6.7
Karstadt	6.0	6.2
Lidl and Schwarz	3.9	5.0
Spar-Group	3.8	4.6
CR5	45.1	45.5
Buying group:		
Markant-Group	11.0	11.3
CR5*	50.0	50.0

Note: Concentration ratio CR5* calculated including Markant-Group and omitting Tengelmann.

Source: Authors' estimates (see Chapter 7).

one major buying group, the Swiss-based Markant group which also has a market share of more than ten per cent. This group acts as a buying group for mostly small independent firms, but also includes some larger players such as the discounter Lidl.

Table 9.4 gives estimates of market concentration by sales in the period 1985–94.[1] As in other European countries, market concentration has increased dramatically in Germany in this period with the five firm concentration ratio almost doubling between 1985 and 1994. Second tier firms are also a key feature in Germany (as noted above) with the second largest five firms accounting for an extra 19 percentage points of concentration in 1994. In our interviews we were told that this group of firms provides a strong 'countervailing' presence to the leading firms, increasing competition further. This contrasts with the UK, for example, where second tier firms are much smaller than the leading firms and tend to have much smaller effects on competition.

Table 9.4 Market concentration by sales (%), 1985–94

	Concentration		
Group	1985	1990	1994
Top 5	31	45	59
Top 10	46	62	78
Others	54	38	22
Total	100	100	100

Source: Schmidt (Wirtschaft und Wettbewerb, 1997).

The rise in concentration in the years 1985–94 is, in part, associated with an increase in merger activity. Prior to 1986 there were significant obstacles to mergers in Germany but these were over-turned in a court ruling in 1986. As a result substantial merger activity developed, especially in 1986–87. Merger activity has also continued into the 1990s although in some cases (e.g. Aldi) firms have developed through internal growth. Some mergers have been cross-national; for example, Rewe's acquisition of the Austrian firms Billa in 1996 and J. Meinl in 1998, and Tengelmann's acquisition of Gruppo PAM in Italy in 1998. Most recently, some large mergers have taken place with Metro buying Allkauf and Kriegbaum, Intermarché buying Spar Handels, and Wal-Mart buying Wertkauf and the larger Spar outlets (>5,000m^2).

Every two years, the Monopolies Commission is required to report on competition and concentration in different industries in Germany. In its 1996/7 report, it found that while mergers continued to take place, resulting in a reduction in the number of medium-sized firms, there was no overall detrimental effect on competition in food retailing. In addition, the growth of discounters, in particular, had kept competition in food retailing very strong.

In 1998, the German Government introduced changes in its Act on Restraints on Competition (Gesetz gegen Wettbewerbsbeschrankungen) to take effect on 1 January 1999. These changes are similar in some respects to those in the 1996 Galland Law in France in that they seek to shift the balance between large multiple retailers and producers/small retailers. First, the new law forbids retailers from setting prices permanently below purchase prices (at the request of suppliers who felt that this affected the consumer's perception of product quality). Second, it allows firms to take action in the courts against the abuse of a dominant position without having to wait for the Cartel Office to take action. Third, it allows suppliers who wish to complain about abuse of purchasing power by a retail chain to remain anonymous during the Cartel Office investigation (although not before the Court). And finally, the law allows exemptions for retail buying groups (with combined market shares of less than 10–15 per cent) from normal cartel laws (intended to enable smaller food retailers to compete with the larger retail chains). These measures show a commitment in German Government to limit the market power of the leading food retailers and to limit possible anti-competitive conduct.

9.2 COMPETITION IN FOOD RETAILING

Although concentration in German food retailing does not seem that out of line with other large member states, the market appears to be more competitive than elsewhere. This provides a warning that concentration data on its own can only provide a first indicator of possible market power and that more detailed analysis is required before strong conclusions can be drawn. In the German case, the growth of discounters has been a major factor in the competitiveness of the retail market.

In terms of the analysis of Chapter 3, the leading multiple chains have buying power (question 1 of Table 3.1), they have it against both powerful and relatively powerless suppliers (question 2) but they do not appear to have significant selling power (at least in some areas: see below) (question 3). This contrasts with the three other countries that we consider. From our analysis, this suggests that while retailers can obtain significant discounts from suppliers, they also tend to pass them on to consumers. According to Schmidt (Wirtschaft und Wettbewerb, 1997), the discounters, in particular, tend to operate on very small margins of only 1–2 per cent compared to typical margins of 6–8 per cent in Spain, 6 per cent in Holland, 6–8 per cent in the UK and 4–6 per cent in France. Moreover, on the products which discounters tend to sell, prices for all food retailers tend to be low because non-discounters are forced to match their prices.

Indeed, many major food retailers have opened their own discount stores to compete for this important segment of the market. And pressure from competition at the retail stage has in turn led to pressure on producers to reduce their margins.

Discounters, such as Aldi, make their profits by concentrating mainly on own label products which are often (but not always) of comparable quality to branded goods. They seek to buy these at the lowest possible prices, and then sell them at a similarly low level. Hence, goods are often displayed in cartons rather than on shelves, they have to be bought in cash or by Eurocheque, and, at the checkouts, operators are expected to memorise the prices in order to avoid delays.[2] Discounters tend to dominate some products (e.g. canned goods) more than others and, typically, offer much less product depth than supermarkets (or hypermarkets). Table 9.5 shows discounter market shares of selected products in 1997.

Table 9.5 Discounters' shares of selected products, 1997

Product	Share of turnover (%)
Canned food	46.7
Chilled food	36.5
Household cleaning products	19.1
Alcoholic drinks	16.0
Fresh food	13.9
Frozen food	13.7
Soft drinks	9.0

Source: Euromonitor, 1998.

9.3 RETAILER AND BUYING GROUP BUYING POWER

The increase in concentration in food retailing in the last 15 years has increased retailer buying power in Germany with each of the companies in Table 9.3 being sufficiently large to exert buying power. Of the leading groups, the Metro group purchases centrally through Metro MGE Einkauf GmbH and does not belong to any buying groups. In contrast, Rewe and Edeka are co-operatively organised and purchase centrally for their members (Einkaufszusammen-schlusse). These groups allow independent supermarket chains to participate in purchasing and hence also act as buying groups. Aldi operates independently and as its own buying group. In contrast, Markant is a straightforward classical buying group in which smaller food retailers group together to obtain the benefit of buying in bulk.

Most food retailers in Germany make use of their size to exert buying power. This is not universally true, however, because Edeka negotiates on a regional basis (with 3 regions) for most products. In fact, it only negotiates at a national level with 7 key suppliers, reflecting the regional nature of the co-operatives which make up this group.

Most of the retailers that we spoke to said that the main factors that they consider in dealing with their suppliers are price and quality. According to one food retail chain, the important factors are the wishes of consumers and the saleability of products. They would not take on a new product even if special payments were offered if they did not think the product would sell or it did not fit in with their store image. On the other hand, for comparable products, the lowest cost supplier would normally win. In addition to price, product quality is an important factor, as is continuity of supply. As leading retailers have faced increasing competition from discounters, they have reacted by developing own brands and opening their own chains of discount stores. Own brands probably account for about ten per cent of the market as a whole (ignoring discounters). These products are often purchased from smaller producers and price is often the key factor.

As in France, bulk buying is an important, but not the only, factor in negotiations between buyers and producers. In most cases, producers are expected to give discounts for purchases in bulk and, in the competitive retail environment, these are typically passed on to consumers in lower prices. In addition, food retailers may charge fees such as listing fees, slotting allowances, fees for promotions, and so on. There is some evidence that retailers may on occasion behave anti-competitively. One example is the case of Metro which, having bought Allkauf in 1998, found that it was receiving more favourable prices on some goods than itself. As a result, Metro tried to renegotiate its contracts retrospectively, although in this case intervention by the Cartel Office stopped this going ahead.

A special feature in Germany has been the reunification of East and West. After reunification, many former East German suppliers had difficulties in becoming listed with West German retailers, and, as these latter spread into the East (with their existing suppliers), East German production came to a standstill. Discounters, in particular, have moved into the East with about 250 new outlets having been opened in 1996 alone. The Government has attempted to overcome the listing problem by helping East German producers to improve product quality and this has enabled some, but by no means all, to be listed by the major chains. Reunification has also been important as other major West German retailers have moved into the East.

Refusal to purchase has been a factor in some cases. Procter & Gamble, for example, in trying to introduce an open pricing policy in Europe for its washing powders in 1996 had products delisted by several major retail chains. Such cases, however, are relatively rare. In some cases, it is very difficult to refuse to purchase especially where a large dominant brand is involved. In such circumstances, retailers have to sell the brand because of customer demand (so-called 'must-stock' brands). Producers with strong brands are also in a stronger position to resist retailers' demands for lower prices, and, we were told, larger brands continue to make high returns for the firms involved.

Smaller suppliers are in a less favourable position and, given the strong retail competition that exists, are under great pressure to reduce their prices.

German companies and buying groups are also members of international alliances. Edeka is a member of AMS (which includes Casino and Safeway), Markant is a member of EMD (with, for example, Britain's Todays group and Spain's Euromadi) and Rewe is a member of Eurogroup. These alliances, we were told, do not appear as yet to have had any major effect as far as retail purchasing power is concerned.

9.4 PRODUCTS

9.4.1 Washing Powders and Detergents

Washing products in Germany are divided into three categories: detergents, softeners and special washing products (e.g. additives for detergents). According to the German retail panel (GFK) sales in January–October 1998 (excluding Aldi) were DM 1.8bn for detergents, DM 0.4bn for softeners and DM 0.6bn for special washing products. Henkel is the largest producer of detergents with 46 per cent of the market, followed by Procter & Gamble with 29 per cent and Unilever with 12 per cent (Table 9.6).

Table 9.6 Market shares (% of sales) for detergents, 1997

Group	Detergents
Henkel	46
Procter & Gamble	29
Unilever	12

Source: Euromonitor, 1998.

Alternative data for detergents from the household panel (which includes Aldi) are shown in Table 9.7. Henkel is the market leader again with 45 per cent of the market, Procter & Gamble is in second place with 26 per cent followed by Unilever with 13 per cent and others (including Aldi with about ten per cent) with 16 per cent. Henkel has increased its market share by 6 percentage points between 1987 and 1997, while Procter & Gamble and Unilever have lost market share in more or less equal proportions – see Table 9.7. Own brands are more successful in Germany than in France (where they account for about 6 per cent of sales), although this is accounted for by Aldi's market share.

The supplier side of the market is dominated (as in France) by a few large firms although the actual ranking differs between them. In France, P&G is the largest firm with about 38 per cent of the market followed by Unilever with 23 per cent and Henkel with 21 per cent. In Germany, however, Henkel, which was formed from a number of separate firms, is the market leader.

Table 9.7 Market shares for detergents, 1987 and 1997

Group	Market share (% of sales)	
	1987	1997
Henkel	39	45
Procter & Gamble	29	26
Unilever	15	13
Others (including Aldi)	16	16

Source: Euromonitor, 1998.

An important feature in this market has been the attempt by P&G to introduce its open pricing policy for its washing products. This sets common prices across Europe, with set discounts for cost savings, etc. Its strategy may be seen as intended to eradicate national bargaining, and, thereby, to avoid the need to give bigger discounts to larger retail chains. Not surprisingly, this policy has been resisted in Germany as well as France, and as a result of this there was a boycott of P&G products by major German retailers. While this lasted for only a few months, the matter was not fully resolved and, at present, P&G still has to negotiate bilaterally with each of the supermarkets and Markant.

Although washing powders are a very basic commodity, there is strong brand allegiance and, with the exception of Aldi, the market is dominated by the three major European firms which rely heavily on advertising to promote their goods. In addition, the major manufacturers produce products for each market segment (standard powders, concentrated powders, etc.) and this makes it difficult for a new producer to enter with only one type of product (e.g. a standard powder). Given the strength of brand allegiances, retailers are limited in the extent to which they can exercise buyer power in this market, although not entirely so as even the largest producers can face the credible threat of being delisted.

9.4.2 Coffee

The major part of the retail coffee market in Germany is roast and ground coffee with annual sales of about DM 8bn. Instant coffee, in contrast, only accounts for ten per cent of retail sales. These figures, in fact, are the exact reverse of those in the UK.

Until recently roast and ground coffee was dominated, on the selling side, by Kraft Jacobs Suchard. However, a merger between Tchibo and Eduscho in 1998 has created an effective duopoly in this market (Table 9.8). KJS has a market share of 30 per cent and Tchibo/Eduscho has a market share of 28 per cent. The market also has two other big players: Albrecht (Aldi) with 18 per cent of the market and Nestlé (with its Dallmeyer brand) with about ten per cent.

Table 9.8 Market shares for roast and ground coffee, 1998

Group	Market share (% of sales)
KJS	30
Tchibo/Eduscho	28
Albrecht (Aldi)	18
Nestlé (Dallmeyer)	10
Others	14

Source: Interviews.

In this market, prices are typically set by negotiation between suppliers and retail chains or buying groups. Given the competitive nature of the downstream market, pressure is put on the major producers to keep prices low in order, in particular, to compete with Albrecht. This implies that an upper limit is put on the prices that major suppliers can charge, notwithstanding their large market shares, and this may be an instance in which competition is quite strong even though the leading firms have large market shares. The market share of Albrecht shows again the strength of discounters in Germany and that consumers are willing to buy a product if it is comparable in quality with the brand leaders, and it is sold at a lower price.

The instant coffee market is much smaller than roast and ground coffee, and the market leader is Nestlé (see Table 9.9). In fact, there are two sub-markets within instant coffee: pure instant coffee (where Nestlé has a much larger market share than 30 per cent) and speciality coffees (e.g. cappuccino), which have grown in importance recently in Germany, and which are dominated by own brands. In this latter market, in particular, discounters have been able to gain market share by reducing prices, and competing directly on price. This contrasts with the UK (see Chapter 11), where own brands and secondary brands are often seen as of inferior quality to branded goods, and hence their market share tends to be quite low. In Germany, consumers have been persuaded that own brands are of sufficient quality, and therefore they appear to compete directly with the major brands.

Table 9.9 Market shares for instant coffee, 1998

Group	Market share (% of sales)
Nestlé	30
KJS	10
Private label and others	62

Source: Interviews

Nestlé does not supply own label products but relies on the strength of its own brands to maintain market share. We were told that there have been instances of de-listing in this sub-market but this is relatively rare. Both the major suppliers (Nestlé and KJS) and the supermarket/buying groups recognise that it is important to have Nestlé (and, to a lesser extent, KJS) brands on their shelves, and this not only prevents de-listing, but also strengthens the bargaining position of the leading brands. Nestlé, in particular, appears to be in a strong position to resist retailer buying power in Germany.

9.4.3 Butter and Margarine

As in France, there are major differences between the butter and margarine markets in Germany. Butter is, essentially, in competitive supply and is often delivered locally from local dairies. On the other hand, production of margarine is dominated by Unilever with a 60 per cent market share (see Table 9.10). Unilever is by a great margin the largest producer with brands such as Rama, Becel and Homa-Gold, while Aldi, in second place, has a much smaller market share of about 13 per cent. The main own brand supplier to Aldi is Rau which accounts for about half of Aldi's 13 per cent market share, and the rest of the market is made up of others (mainly own brands).

Unilever is clearly in a strong position in this market, and this helps it in resisting demands for price discounts. Very few food retailers (apart from discounters) could risk de-listing Unilever's products, although this has apparently happened occasionally in the past. Hence, while buying power is important in Germany, Unilever is probably able to resist pressure to reduce prices to a considerable degree, although smaller producers are in a considerably weaker position.

Table 9.10 Market shares for margarine, 1998

Group	Market share (% of sales)
UDL (Unilever)	60
Aldi	13
Others (mainly own brands)	27

Source: Interviews.

One new feature in the market has been the attempt by some retailers to demand a Euro-bonus (in the form of an additional discount of 3 per cent) related to the total of their purchases of margarine across Europe. This bonus is not related specifically to any cost savings in handling goods. It seems likely, in the future, that more demands of this type will be made by food retailers as international alliances grow stronger and as food retail companies expand abroad.

Margins for own brand suppliers of margarine appear very low in Germany and, in some cases, so low that they may not even be able to cover their costs. In this part of the market, purchases are put out to tender and usually the lowest price wins. Quality, of course, is also a factor, but given an acceptable level of quality, sales usually go to the lowest bidder.

It seems likely that Unilever will continue to dominate the market in Germany, in part by introducing new products (such as margarine with olive oil), and also because of its strong brands. Own brand market shares may, however, increase to some extent, and retail buyer concentration is also likely to rise.

Butter is a slightly smaller market in Germany than margarine and, as noted above, appears to be very competitive. The largest brand is probably Kerrygold (from Ireland) with a market share of about ten per cent, but the market mainly consists of small producers and own brands. Since the quality of butter is defined by law, supermarkets and buying groups mainly buy on price, and this means that suppliers' margins can be very low – we were told of the order of less than one per cent, compared to 6 per cent in the UK and up to ten per cent elsewhere. This side of the market is, therefore, very similar to own brand sales of margarine.

NOTES

1. These estimates are not directly comparable with those in Table 9.3.
2. In contrast to most other food retailers, Aldi do not use scanners and this accounts for them often being excluded from analyses of food retailing which use scanner data.

10. Food Retailing in Spain

10.1 MARKET STRUCTURE CHARACTERISTICS AND EVOLUTION

Food retailers are the most important single component of Spanish retail sales, covering 44.5 per cent of the total retail market in 1996. Over the last decade the structure and organisation of food retailing has changed considerably, with the market becoming technological, sophisticated and increasingly concentrated. The dominant players have become the hypermarket and supermarket groups which have increased both in number and average size, selling a large variety of food and non-food products and offering a variety of additional services to consumers.

The market is divided between five main kinds of player:

- hypermarkets (with sales areas in excess of 2,500 sq. m., long uninterrupted trading hours, large free parking facilities and 40 per cent of sales devoted to sales of non-food products);
- large supermarkets (sales areas over 400 sq. m., 70 per cent of which, on average, is dedicated to food retail distribution);
- small supermarkets (sales areas around 250–400 sq. m and at least two tills);
- convenience stores; and
- independent retailers.

Due to differences in ownership (which will be discussed later), it is necessary to distinguish between the hypermarket and supermarket sectors, and then between large and small supermarkets. As shown in Table 10.1, the hypermarkets dominated the market in 1995 with 33 per cent of total food turnover, more than doubling their market share in 1987–95. Both large and small supermarkets have increased their market share over the period but to a smaller extent (by 17 per cent and 24 per cent respectively). On the other hand, convenience stores and, in particular, small, independent retailers, have suffered a continuous decrease in market share (by 38 per cent and 62 per cent respectively).

135

Table 10.1 Market shares in Spanish food retailing by outlet type (% of sales value), 1987–95

	1987	1988	1989	1990	1991	1992	1993	1994	1995
Hypermarkets	15	18	20	23	26	29	31	31	33
Large Supermarkets	12	12	12	12	12	12	12	13	14
Small Supermarkets	25	27	29	30	30	30	31	31	31
Convenience Stores	16	16	15	15	14	13	13	12	10
Independent Retailers	32	27	24	20	18	16	15	13	12

Source: Distribucion y Consumo, Diciembre-Enero, 1996.

The level and change in concentration in food and the fast moving goods sector is shown in Table 10.2. The table shows that the five biggest retail groups in the Spanish food retailing sector controlled 32.6 per cent of the market in 1996: Promodès (9.7 per cent), Pryca (7.1. per cent), Eroski (6.3 per cent), Alcampo (5.1 per cent), and Hipercor (4.4 per cent). Promodès increased its market share by two percentage points in 1993–6 while Pryca's market share

Table 10.2 Concentration in food retailing, 1993 and 1996

	1993 (%)	1996 (%)
Promodès	7.8	9.7
Pryca (Carrefour)	6.9	7.1
Eroski	3.2	6.3
Alcampo (Auchan)	3.6	5.1
Hipercor (El Corte Inglés	2.4	4.4
CR5	23.9	32.6

Source: Authors' estimates (see Chapter 7).

increased slightly and the other three leading firms also increased their market share. Five-firm concentration increased from 23.9 per cent in 1993 to 32.6 per cent per cent in 1996. While the main business of all of these groups is in hypermarkets, Table 10.3 shows that all the groups enjoy a direct or indirect presence in the supermarket or discounter business.

Promodès, Pryca and Alcampo are French owned: Pryca's main shareholder is Carrefour BV, Promodès' main shareholder is Promodès France, and Alcampo's leading shareholder is the Auchan group. Carrefour entered the Spanish market in 1973, Promodès in 1976 and Auchan in 1979. The other two major chains are Spanish owned, with Hipercor a subsidiary of the major Spanish retailing group, El Corte Inglés.

Table 10.3 Composition of the main groups in the Spanish FMCG industry

Group	
Grupo Promodès	Continente, Dia, Punto-Cash, Punto de la Plata, Iliturgitana, Simago
Pryca	Pryca, through Comptoirs Modernes (Comodisa, Maxor, Supermercats Economics)
Gidae	Eroski, Syp, Unide, Cenco, Becodis, La Merced
Grupo Alcampo	Alcampo, Sabeco
El Corte Inglés	Hipercor, Supermercados El Corte Inglés

Source: Interviews.

While five firm concentration is lower in Spain than in the other countries in this study, it is clear that it is growing at a rapid rate. A key feature in this has been the expansion of the French retail chains in Spain. In a relatively short space of time (since the mid-1970's), French groups (in particular, Promodès) have built up a strong position in Spain. While much of this has been by direct investment in out-of-town hypermarkets, mergers and take-overs have also been important. Some of the principal take-overs in the period 1996–8 are shown in Table 10.4.

Table 10.4 Principal mergers and take-overs, 1996–98

	Acquired company	Acquiring company
1996	Jumbo (Pan de Azucar)	Alcampo
1996	Expresso (Pan de Azucar)	Alcampo
1997	Almacenes Gomez Serrano	Mercadona
1997	Unide/Mercat	Eroski
1997	Sabeco	Alcampo
1997	Simago	Promodès
1998	Hilario Osorio	Unigro

Source: Interviews.

Although the growth of hypermarkets and large supermarkets has been beneficial to consumers as a whole, concern has been expressed in Spain over their effect on small retailers and suppliers. This resulted in the passing of the 1996 Commerce Law (Ley de Regulacion del Comercio Minorista) which aims to limit the market power of the major retail groups. Its main provisions are:-

- except in the regions of Valencia, Catalunya and Galicia, two levels of authorisation are now required for the construction of out-of-town supermarkets or hypermarkets: a planning and zoning permit from the local authority and an authorisation from the regional government which is based on existing coverage and retail saturation levels. This has complicated enormously the opening of new outlets. Although this can be seen to be a limiting factor in the hypermarket expansion process, it also gives a strategic advantage for the incumbents and acts as a barrier to entry to new competitors. There is also evidence that some of the major chains have in the past bought large, cheaper sites in excess of their needs, and now enjoy a serious advantage by not selling/renting them, or renting them only at very high prices.
- to limit hypermarket opening hours (especially restricting Sunday opening to eight Sundays in a year). The immediate consequence of this has been further price cuts by the hypermarkets to recover the loss of Sunday sales.
- to prevent selling below cost. The effect of this is to prevent hypermarkets from pricing their best selling items below cost, and it is expected that it will enable smaller stores to regain a competitive position.
- to prevent retailers and buying organisations stretching the term of payment to suppliers. Delaying payments represents receiving finance without interest which arguably has been used by the retail chains both to operate in the financial markets and to finance their expansion process. It follows that a hypermarket group which is able to invest efficiently in the financial markets could be profitable even when setting prices below costs. The 1996 Law stipulates that any payment delayed by more than 90 days will require a letter of credit, and any payment delayed more than 120 days is subject to a possible demand for a banker's reference by the supplier. However, the real effects of the regulation have been limited and terms of payment to suppliers of the big chains (in 1997 they were, on average, 118.33 days for Continente, Pryca and Alcampo) are still well above the average of northern European countries.

Although the 1996 Commerce Law is expected to slow down the rate of closure of independent food retail outlets, the overall trend is a continuous reduction in their number, and an increase in the degree of concentration of the Spanish food retail market.

However, domestic firms have been active in their response to the advance of foreign-owned hypermarket groups. For example, ARDE (Asociacion para la Reforma de la Distribucion Espanola) was formed by some 30 small and medium-sized supermarket chains to lobby on behalf of Spanish-owned businesses. At the same time, Alcampo, Pryca and Continente formed Instituto de Estudios de Libre Comercio as a lobbying group, with Eroski being represented, to seek to limit the extent of legislation.

Another important element for the future configuration of the market is the possible expansion of the discounters, which could significantly affect the supermarket sector. Whereas it is expected that the strategy of the small supermarkets will be to add discount outlets or to convert existing ones to discounting, it is very likely that the strategy of the larger supermarket chains will be expansion via the opening of new outlets or acquisition of smaller local chains, a strategy which they have followed in the past in order to control both out-of-town and in-town locations.

10.2 RETAILER BUYING POWER

In Spain, the major food retailers are not part of buying groups. Rather the leading food retailers use their own buying power to extract discounts from suppliers. (There are, however, also two leading buying groups with 44 per cent of sales – see below). Retailers, on average, account for between ten per cent and 20 per cent of the sales of large manufacturing companies and more than 25 per cent of the sales of small and medium-sized companies. In addition, retailers control the shelf-space available to producers and are increasingly introducing own brand products which compete with branded lines.

Table 10.5 Figures for aggregated balances, 1997

	Aggregated balances of Pryca, Continente and Alcampo	Aggregated balances of other 800 distributors
Operational costs (% of total revenue)	15.84	16.04
Point-of-sale turnover (days)	40.68	40.52
Gross margin (% of total revenue)	19.29	16.16

Note: Figures include some other goods such as white line appliances.

Source: Registro Mercanti, 1998.

Table 10.5 shows the operational costs, revenues and gross margins of three of the top retailers, with the average for the rest. There is no significant difference in operating costs or point-of-sale turnover in this comparison, but gross margins of the larger hypermarket chains are more than three percentage points higher than the rest. This indicates that while these chains have been able to extract large discounts from suppliers, they have failed to pass at least some of these lower costs on to consumers.

The large food retailers take their purchasing decisions on the basis of a two step procedure. In the first stage, the supermarket carries out a selection among prospective candidates using as criteria price, interest in the brand, guarantee of supply, and so on. The second and most interesting step is the elaboration of what is commonly called the 'plantillas', in which the retailer makes explicit the concrete conditions of the supply relationship. The standard conditions of these supply contracts are the following:

- a listing fee which is paid simply for store presence;
- slotting allowances;
- additional monetary sums to locate products in end-of-aisle displays;
- fixed end-of-year rebates: payments in advance of variable compensation linked to volumes of sales achieved;
- demands for long terms of payment that do not match product turnover. Cruz, Fernandez and Rebollo (1997) show that the length of the term of payment is directly related to the size of the distributor;
- return of unsold units (especially relevant for fresh food and vegetables);
- contributions to special promotions such as 'three for two deals';
- small and local manufacturers either have to pay a fee to a hypermarket to refill the shelves with their products or have to do it themselves.

From the configuration of the supply contracts specified above it is clear that the discounts obtained by hypermarkets from their suppliers are not simply associated with cost savings. The hypermarket groups obtain discounts making explicit use of their bargaining power when negotiating with suppliers, and obtain reductions that are not related to buying in bulk.

We were also told of a number of practices in Spanish food retailing which more clearly emphasise the exercise of buyer power.

- contributions to store openings, remodelling and extensions. Examples are:
  - one of the Pryca 'plantilla' sheets says: 'The firm XXXX will pay to each new store opened during 1996 the amount of XXXX Ptas as an opening contribution. This amount will be debited directly from the supplier account.'
  - in February 1996, Simago (Promodès group) required from its suppliers one per cent of their sales in 1995 because of economic

problems and to finance store reconstruction (*El Pais*, 18 February 1996).
- Dia (Promodès group) required a contribution of between 10,000 and 50,000 Ptas for each of the Dirsa stores it refurbished to give them the Dia format.
- Alcosto (associated with the IFA buying group) asked suppliers to give a percentage retroactive discount on 1993 sales to finance its expansion (*Cinco Dias*, 25 February 1997).
- retroactive discounts over sales in the previous period in the event of mergers, acquisitions ('wedding gifts') or anniversaries. Examples:
  - Alcampo after buying Jumbo and Sabeco in March 1996 asked suppliers for a retroactive discount of one per cent of the previous year's sales (*Cinco Dias*, 4 November 1998)
  - Eroski after agreement with Unide and Mercat, under the threat of de-listing, required from their suppliers three million Ptas or a two per cent discount on 1997 sales (*Expansion*, 3 February 1998, *Cinco Dias*, 4 November 1998)
  - Continente (Promodès group) after acquiring Simago in 1998 required from suppliers a one per cent or two per cent discount on total sales in 1998 (*Cinco Dias*, 4 November 1998)
  - examples of requirements for anniversary discounts are the IFA buying group in 1997 (*Cinco Dias*, 5 February 1997) and Sidamsa (central buying arm of the Promodès group) also in 1997.
- unilateral increases in discounts without compensation for suppliers.
- application of a regressive end-of-year rebate to penalise those suppliers that did not reach target levels of sales.
- 'exclusive purchase' arrangements which are common practice for the supply of private labels.

On the face of it, these practices go beyond what one would normally expect in a straightforward trading relationship and must give cause for concern.

Also in Spain, in particular, another practice needs to be considered. While in most northern European countries terms of payment for food and household goods are generally between as little as nine and 12 days, the term of payment of the largest Spanish distributors are sometimes as long as 120 days. This length of payment is extremely long if compared to an average point-of-sale turnover of between seven and 20 days. The possible repercussions of these delays in the Spanish FMCG industry are:-

- an increase in the costs of Spanish manufacturers relative to other European manufacturers who do not experience these delays;

- a drain on manufacturing funds, limiting the possibility of investment in new product development and productivity improvements;
- in the opinion of the manufacturers, a latent financial risk given the possibility of retailer bankruptcy. (An example given to us of this potential threat was the bankruptcy of two major retailers: Digsa and Mas por Menos).

The Alcampo, Eroski and Continente retroactive discount episodes described above have been investigated by the Comision de Seguimiento del Observatorio de la Distribucion Comercial (Observatory of Commercial Distribution). They concluded that the requirement of payments greater than indicated in the contract signed between supplier and retailer could be considered a unilateral and retrospective violation of the contractual conditions and therefore not binding by law. These practices could also be considered as an abuse of a dominant position and so could be referred to the Tribunal de Defensa de la Competencia (Defence of Competition Office).

10.3 BUYING GROUPS

The number and importance of buying groups has increased over the past decade. They are, typically, made up of predominantly independent and smaller retailers seeking to obtain buying economies, to compete more effectively with the major chains. As shown in Table 10.6, the two leading buying groups are

Table 10.6 Market shares of retailers and buying groups, 1996

Group	Market Shares %
Supermarket Groups	
Promodès	9.7
Pryca	7.1
Eroski	6.3
Alcampo	5.1
Hipercor & Supermercados El Corte Inglés	4.4
CR5	32.6
Buying Groups	
Euromadi (excludes Syp and Simago)	22.2
IFA	22.1
CR5*	67.4

Note: Concentration ratio CR5* calculated omitting Alcampo and Hipercor.

Source: Authors' estimates (see Chapter 7).

Euromadi and IFA with market shares of 22.2 and 22.1 per cent respectively in 1996. These groups account for much larger market shares than even Promodès (9.7 per cent) and Pryca (7.1 per cent). In addition, Eroski is a member of the Gidae buying group with Syp, Unide and Cenco-Becodis La Merced.

Table 10.7 shows the most significant members of IFA and Euromadi in terms of sales and percentage of Pryca's sales. As can be seen, these chains are, individually, much smaller than Pryca, and typically represent small to medium-sized supermarket chains. A significant number of these firms have sales of around Ptas 100 billion. The main aim of these firms is to obtain discounts from suppliers to enable them to compete with the leading retail chains; in addition, some mergers have also taken place, as, for example, in the recent merger of Enaco and Ahorramas.

Table 10.7 Size and leading members of buying groups, 1996

		Sales 1996 in Billion Pts	% of Pryca sales
IFA	GIC-AIE	125	21.0
	Caprabo	90	15.1
	Superdipol	90	15.1
	Enaco-Ahorramas	83	13.9
	Osoro-Uvesco	62	10.4
Euromadi	Syp	102	17.1
	Unigro	92	15.4
	Simago	70	11.8

Source: AC Nielsen, 1998.

The major food retailers also have an indirect relationship with the main buying groups as shown in Table 10.8.

Although the major buying groups represent smaller chains, they also have restrictions on who can join: for example, Grupo IFA requires a minimum annual turnover of Ptas ten billion, and other factors such as common interest and performance are also taken into account. This suggests that smaller retailers may have to merge (or be taken over) in order to survive in the short to medium term.

It was reported to us that Euromadi and IFA perform broadly similar tasks in terms of their central buying activity in that they (i) negotiate rebates, (ii) agree purchase prices, (iii) agree payment terms, (iv) agree promotional activity,

Table 10.8 Penetration by major retailers of buying groups

	Description
Continente	Promodès owns 34% of Ilurgitana de Hipermerados, while 66% belongs to Luis Piña S.A., a member of Euromadi.
Continente	Promodès acquired Simago, associated to Euromadi.
Pryca	Carrefour now owns Comptoirs Modernes (which controls Comodisa, Maxor and Supermercats Economics, associated with IFA).
Mercadona	Merger agreement with Gomez Serrano, a member of Euromadi.
Eroski	Creation of Gidae, in association with Syp and Unide.

Source: Interviews.

and (v) act as the payment point. While individual members also undertake some of these activities on their own behalf (e.g. negotiating rebates, purchase prices and promotional activity), they are left to agree range, listing and dispatch conditions, generate orders, and be the delivery and invoice point.

10.4 OWN BRANDS

Own brands are becoming increasingly important in Spanish retailing, and in food retailing in particular. The market share of own brands in retailing in 1994 is estimated at 8.3 per cent with a higher penetration for food products (11.1 per cent) than for non-food products (6.7 per cent). Although this is low compared with own brand penetration in the UK (37 per cent in 1996), it is growing fast, nearly doubling in 1990–94.

The role and importance of own brand products has drastically changed in the 1990's. Whereas they were first introduced in supermarkets as a cheap and low-quality alternative to branded products, with the aim of stimulating sales especially during a recession, in the last few years major retailer own brands are characterised by an increasing degree of sophistication and a deeper market penetration. Since 1990 own brand products have increasingly been used both to compete with branded products, and to create loyalty to the supermarket.

The approach to own brand production varies across manufacturers, especially among those who already produce major brands. Some of them have opened up to the market for own labels, whereas others base their strategy (and advertising) on the very fact of not producing own brands. Among the companies that do not produce own brands (as they consider them harmful to their reputation), are Kelloggs, Coca-Cola and Gillette. Brand producers involved in the production of own brands include Danone, McCain, Mahou (a subsidiary of Guinness), Casera (the brand leader in the Spanish lemonade industry) and Campofrio (the brand leader in the Spanish roast ham industry).

A phenomenon relevant from the marketing point of view is that Hipercor specifies on its own brand products the name of the producer. If we consider that own brand products are located on the shelves close to branded products, that they look very similar and that they are 10 per cent to 20 per cent cheaper, the fact that the consumer can identify the producer, if well known, makes the marketing advantage of own brand products evident.

We were told that own brand product margins are, typically, greater than branded product margins. There are two reasons for this. On the one hand, retailer bargaining power is greater when negotiating the wholesale price of own brand products; on the other, because own brand products are unique to each retailer, they offer some protection from direct retailer-to-retailer competition.

Furthermore, in Spain branded products appear to have repeatedly been used as the main competitive category to build a customer base, having been sold at a very low adjusted price (or even at loss) in order to attract consumers to particular groups.

Because they contribute to making the threat of de-listing credible, own brand products strengthen the bargaining power of the retailers if they are perceived as a close alternative to branded products. It is difficult to find direct evidence on this, but this argument may be linked with the 'wedding gift' requested by Eroski at the time of the creation of Gidae, because it was apparently made under the threat of de-listing.

It is also worth noting the effect of the increasing importance of own brands on the decline of secondary brands. These products, which used to be cheaper alternatives to the main brands, have in many cases disappeared from the retailers' shelves. The reason is twofold: on the one hand, secondary brands are unable to compete on price with own brand products (due to their need to support their brands through promotions); on the other hand, sometimes they have been delisted by the supermarket chains because they could not match the conditions requested by the retailers. For some of these secondary brand producers the only alternative has been the conversion to own brand production.

10.5 PRODUCTS

10.5.1 Washing Powders and Detergents

The Spanish market for washing powders and detergents is a mature market and laundry detergents are considered low-cost, low-margin, volume shifting goods.

In order to obtain a picture of the importance of this product in Spain compared to other EU markets, Table 10.9 shows the average per capita expenditure on textile washing products in 1997 for various countries. Inspection of Table 10.9 shows that the average per capita expenditure of textile washing products in Spain is intermediate between other EU countries. The average expenditure in Spain (25.97 ecus) is similar to that in France (25.39 ecus) but lower than the average expenditure in the UK and Italy (27.80 and 30.72 ecus respectively).

Table 10.9 Average per capita expenditure on textile washing products in ecus (1997 exchange rates)

Country	Average per capita expenditure (in ecus)
Italy	30.72
UK	27.80
Spain	25.97
France	25.39
Germany	23.89

Source: Market Research Europe, July 1998.

The total size of the Spanish market in 1997 was Ptas 98.35 bn, down from Ptas 103.31 bn in 1993, representing a decrease in the real value of sales of 4.8 per cent. This is similar to other European countries such as Italy, Germany and Benelux. The main factors explaining it are:

- competition among leading manufacturers has restricted the (value) growth of sales. Many companies, such as Procter & Gamble, have been forced to reduce prices and/or offer special promotions to compete;
- consumers have moved back from more expensive concentrated powders to cheaper standard powders;
- there has been increasing market penetration by own brands and discount stores.

The Spanish market for washing products is dominated by 4 large firms: Henkel and P&G who each have about 20 per cent of sales, followed by Benckiser with 17 per cent and Unilever with 13 per cent. The key brands are listed in Table 10.10. In addition, own brand shares account for a further 14 per cent of sales. The market is quite similar to that in other EU countries (although the mix of market shares varies from country to country) and prices and terms and conditions are, again, determined by negotiation between the major firms or buying groups on each side of the market.

Table 10.10 Main producers and washing powder brands

Groups	Brands
Benckiser	Colon, Elena, Vial
Henkel	Blancol, Dixan, Micolor, Mistolin, Perlan, Wipp
P&G	Ariel, Dash
Unilever	Luzil, Skip

Source: Market Research in Europe, July 1998.

A major feature of the Spanish market is the importance of the two buying groups, Euromadi and IFA, in addition to the major food retail chains. These groups, of course, represent many independent retailers and, through mergers, parts of the leading supermarket chains. The evidence we collected in Spain suggests that sales by leading manufacturers to the leading five supermarket chains were of the order of 40 per cent of total sales, and that a similar figure also applies to the buying groups. If buying groups are, therefore, included with the leading supermarket chains, producers are heavily dependent on these groups (and chains). Not surprisingly, the producers we contacted felt that buying power was a very important problem for them.

We have already highlighted some of the practices in retailing in Spain which might be considered as manifestations of buyer power. In this sector, as elsewhere, we again heard comments on the term of payment of supermarket chains in Spain which often exceeds 100 days, and is much longer than in the northern Europe. In addition, retroactive discounts, 'wedding gifts', and so on were also mentioned as a problem. These problems, in fact, appear to be fairly widespread in Spain and were also raised in the two other product groups discussed below.

10.5.2 Coffee

Instant coffee accounts for a relatively small part of the Spanish coffee market, with sales predominantly consisting of roast and ground coffee. The emphasis on roast and ground coffee has allowed a number of suppliers to establish quite strong market positions, but with no particular dominant firm and overall concentration is relatively low.

Consumption of coffee in Spain has been fairly constant at about 70,000 tonnes per annum over recent years. The real value of sales of coffee took a dip, however, in the early 1990s (to around Ptas 48bn per annum) before increasing in the mid 1990s (to around Ptas 55bn). These changes, however, reflect changes in the world price of coffee rather than dramatic changes in consumption.

Table 10.11 shows per capita sales of coffee (in ecus per capita) in several EU countries. In this group, Spain has relatively low consumption of coffee, similar to that in the UK, but much less than in Italy or France.

Three companies had market shares in excess of 10 per cent in 1996: Nestlé (producing instant coffee) and Douwe Egberts and Kraft Jacobs Suchard. Nestlé is the leader in the Spanish coffee sector in terms of production, with a volume share of about 16 per cent in 1995 with its Nescafé and Bonka brands. The second and third players in the market, Douwe-Egberts (Marcilla) and KJS, have about 12 per cent and 11 per cent respectively and specialise in the roast and ground coffee sector. The rest of the market (over 60 per cent) is, however, accounted for by small suppliers and own brands.

Table 10.11 Per capita value of sales (ecus per capita) of coffee, 1995

Country	Per capita value of sales (ecus)
FRANCE	18.23
ITALY	18.12
UK	12.36
SPAIN	11.33

Source: Consumer Europe, 1995.

While there are leading producers in Spain, the supply-side of the market is relatively unconcentrated. Under these circumstances, both retailer buying power and competition between firms can lead to lower prices and low margins. A leading trade organisation told us that both large and small suppliers are continually under pressure from leading retail groups and buying groups to reduce prices in this sector, and that this, in turn, puts pressure on them to reduce their costs. Leading producers have an advantage over smaller producers in that consumers want to buy their brands, allowing them to resist buyer pressure to some extent. Smaller producers, however, do not enjoy this luxury and, for them, competition appears to be very strong.

10.5.3 Butter and Margarine

The traditional Mediterranean diet in Spain is characterised by high consumption of vegetable oil (especially olive oil) and by low levels of consumption of saturated fats. This is illustrated in Table 10.12 which compares per capita consumption of butter and margarine across several EU countries. Spanish consumption of butter is only one tenth of the level in, say, Italy or the UK, and only about one thirtieth of that in Germany and France. On the other hand, consumption of margarine is lower in Italy than in Spain, although, again, consumption in the UK and Germany is much higher than in Spain.

With respect to the relative importance of butter and margarine in total yellow fats sales, margarine predominates. The relative share of this product has, though, been decreasing over recent years, but it still accounts for around 70 per cent of total yellow fats sales.

Table 10.12   Per capita value of sales (ecus per capita) of butter and margarine, 1995

Country	Butter	Margarine
France	18.19	6.11
Germany	21.67	17.11
Italy	7.72	0.68
UK	6.75	11.71
Spain	0.79	2.12

Source: Consumer Europe, 1995.

The evolution of the sales of margarine and butter in Spain over the period 1990–95 is shown in Table 10.13. This table shows a decline in the sales of margarine both in volume (-30.61 per cent) and in real and current value (-40.62 per cent and -22.20 per cent respectively).

In contrast, sales of butter both in volume and in current value increased during the period (+40 per cent and +17.61 per cent respectively). An increasing preference for butter and some confusion over the relative healthiness of butter and margarine seem to have been factors underlying this change. This increase in volume and current sales value of butter has been accompanied by a decrease in the real sales value of butter (-10.33 per cent), which seems to have been provoked by competition and, in particular, by the low-price policy of Pascual (the leading producer of butter in Spain) together with the increasing importance of own brand products.

The butter market in Spain is dominated by local (Spanish) manufacturers. In 1995, the market leader, Pascual, had a 19 per cent market share, followed by Arias with 14 per cent and CLAS with 13 per cent. Other firms with notable market shares include Puleva with about seven per cent of the market and Remy Picot with about three per cent, with own brands accounting for a further 13 per cent of the market, and the remaining third being taken by smaller independent firms.

Table 10.13 Sales of margarine and butter, 1990–95

	Margarine			Butter		
	'000 Tonnes	Ptas Billions	Ptas Billions (1990 prices)	'000 Tonnes	Ptas Billions	Ptas Billions (1990 prices)
1990	49	17.21	17.21	5	4.26	4.26
1991	51	18.07	16.94	5	4.56	4.27
1992	51	17.75	15.71	5	4.44	3.92
1993	45	16.78	14.03	6	5.16	4.31
1994	37	14.34	11.45	7	5.14	4.10
1995	34	13.39	10.22	7	5.01	3.82
Change[1]	-30.61	-22.20	-40.62	+40	+17.61	-10.33

Note: [1] Per cent change.

Source: Consumer Europe, 1995.

In the margarine market, Agra (a subsidiary of Unilever) is the leading producer with its Tulipan and Flora brands.

Competition in the butter market has been intense in recent years in particular, because the leading grocery chains set low prices for leading brands to attract consumers into their stores. This has led to strong downward pressure on prices in the butter case. As far as margarine is concerned, pressure is of another sort: namely, the substantial fall in demand that appears to have taken place. This has also led to pressure on prices, although in this case Unilever would appear to have been better able to resist. Supermarket buying power is also regarded as important in this sector, although probably more so for smaller manufacturers than for Unilever itself.

11. United Kingdom Food Retailing

11.1 MARKET STRUCTURE CHARACTERISTICS AND EVOLUTION

Food retailing is the single most important component of UK retail sales, with 47 per cent of the total market in 1997. The last twenty years have witnessed an enormous change in its structure and organisation. This has shifted the market from being rather unsophisticated into being highly technological, sophisticated and concentrated. Large multiple stores have become dominant, selling a variety of food and non-food products, and offering many additional services to their customers.

The retail market can be divided into three main groups:

- large multiple stores;
- smaller multiple stores (including symbol groups[1] and convenience stores) and discounters;
- independent retailers and specialist outlets.

Table 11.1 shows the market share of these types of outlet. Independent retailers have lost market share in 1992–97, while multiple stores have increased their share. By 1997, two thirds of all sales were made through multiples, showing the strong position of these stores in the UK.

Table 11.1 Market share evolution, 1992–97

	1992	1993	1994	1995	1996	1997
Large multiples	62.9	64.3	66.0	65.9	65.6	67.0
Smaller multiples	16.0	16.1	16.2	16.2	16.2	16.1
Discounters	8.4	7.5	5.7	6.5	6.6	6.2
Independents	10.4	9.4	9.3	8.6	8.0	7.3
Off licences	2.3	2.6	2.8	2.8	3.6	3.4
Total	100	100	100	100	100	100

Source: Euromonitor/ONS/trade estimates.

An additional viewpoint is given in Table 11.2, which shows the dominance of five leading multiple groups. In this table, the five leading firms had 56 per cent of sales in 1996, higher than in France and Germany, and much higher than in Spain. Other supermarket groups (not included in the table) are much smaller, with only Kwik Save having a market share above four per cent, while independent co-operative retail stores, as a group, also had 5.0 per cent of sales in 1997.

Table 11.2 shows the development of market shares in the UK for 1993–96. Clearly the four major firms dominate the market with Tesco and Sainsbury being considerably larger than the third and fourth ranked firms (Asda and Safeway). There is, therefore, a clear asymmetric oligopoly in the UK market. Other firms are considerably smaller with Somerfield, the fifth ranked firm, having a market share of only 4.5 per cent in 1996.

Table 11.2 Market shares, 1993 and 1996

Group	1993 (%)	1996 (%)
Tesco	13.7	18.5
Sainsbury	14.8	14.2
Asda	7.9	9.7
Safeway	9.2	9.3
Somerfield	4.8	4.5
CR5	50.4	56.2

Source: Authors' estimates (see Chapter 7).

Concentration has also increased markedly in the 1993–96 period with the major multiples pursuing active policies of new store development. Over this period Tesco has overtaken Sainsbury to become the market leader and, more recently, has taken a more commanding lead.[2] Asda also gained significant market share in the period, rising from eight per cent in 1993 to nearly ten per cent in 1996, taking it from the fourth to the third largest food retailer.[3]

The main reasons for these changes can be summarised as follows:

Cost and demand advantages:

- Larger stores can stock and sell many more products, which is consistent with consumer preferences;
- cost advantages from the existence of buying power (see below);
- economies of scale and scope in logistics and distribution. Wholesaling and distribution are internalised, and the retailer controls them directly. Suppliers now transport much of their merchandise to a centralised depot

which then allocates it to the outlets. New technology, with fridge and freezer capacity, enables the retail chains to transport in a single journey many different items to each outlet, reducing the number of journeys and therefore reducing costs;

- technological progress. The adoption of EPOS (electronic point of sale), EFTPS (electronic funds transfer systems) and electronic scanners have greatly improved the efficiency of distribution and stocking activities, with needs being communicated almost in real time to the supplier.

Legal and institutional advantages:

- at the beginning of the decade it was relatively easy to obtain planning permission to build out-of-town stores, but the recent tightening up of planning regulations makes it much more difficult to obtain permission, providing a strategic advantage to incumbent firms;
- Partly as a result of the Sunday Trading Act 1994, late-night opening (with a few stores having 24-hour opening) and Sunday opening have become the rule for the large multiples, weakening the position of smaller retailers operating as convenience stores.

Strategic advantages:

- related to consumer loyalty, reputation and advertising have an effect of restricting the residual demand for a potential entrant;
- The four major multiples are now investing heavily in building retail brands and consumer loyalty, through the use of loyalty cards and the spread of their own brand products. Loyalty cards additionally provide the retailer with detailed information on consumer tastes and changing preferences.

Social changes:

- Over time, British customers have moved towards one-stop shopping and bulk shopping. This, in turn, is due to a variety of social changes (e.g. increased use of cars, more women going to work, and so on). Also supermarkets have increased the amount of non-food items sold (about 27 per cent of their total turnover in 1997) including books, music and clothes.

These factors have served to allow the major retailers a competitive advantage over their smaller rivals. The indication is that the market will concentrate further, with the large multiple stores increasing their shares through new store openings, and possibly through mergers.

11.2 RETAILER BUYING AND SELLING POWER

In Chapter 7 the UK market was characterised as a duopoly in which the two leading firms have significantly higher market shares than other leading firms. Nevertheless, the two second ranked firms (Asda and Safeway) also have close to a ten per cent market share, and the five firm concentration ratio (56 per cent in 1996) is the highest of the four countries we have considered in Part III.

Consistent with their size and position in the market, the leading four retail groups appear to have significant buying power over suppliers. This has manifested itself partly as a way of increasing efficiency, and partly in their ability to negotiate price discounts and other favourable terms and conditions. There is no doubt that consumers have gained from the development of supermarket chains in the UK in the form of higher quality products, easier one-stop shopping, more choice and lower prices. Nevertheless, concerns have been expressed about supermarket buying (and selling) power in the UK and its effects on economic welfare. Three issues have come to the fore and are discussed below:

- The prices and profitability of supermarkets in the UK;
- Possible monopsony power, in particular in relation to UK farmers; and
- Fees and rebate schemes.

11.2.1 Supermarket Prices and Profits

The first issue concerns the ability of UK retail grocery chains to set prices high and earn monopoly profits. Claims have been made that supermarket chains in the UK use their buying power to obtain substantial discounts from suppliers, but then fail to pass them on to consumers.

Evidence of high prices has been given, for example, by a leading Sunday newspaper (*The Sunday Times*) which ran a campaign in 1998–99 to show that UK food prices are much higher than in other countries in Europe, and in the US. Using a typical basket of goods (and an index with the UK set at 100), it found that prices were just 61 in the Netherlands, 62 in Belgium, 74 in France, 65 in Germany and 69 in the US. Such comparisons, however, need to be treated with care.[4] In the UK, for example, taxes are higher on some goods (notably alcohol) than they are in some other European countries and in the US. In addition, consumers in the UK tend to consume more own brand goods (which are typically not included in such comparisons), and the exchange rate has been high. This raises a note of caution, therefore, although the prima facie evidence seems quite strong.

This issue was also looked at by the UK Competition Commission (2000). In its report, it found that, allowing for tax and quality differences, UK food prices were about 12–16 per cent higher than those in France, Germany and the Netherlands in late 1999. However, part of this, they argued was due to the high exchange rate, and higher land and building costs in the UK.[5] They did not find evidence of excessive pricing in the UK although, arguably, they were not able to explain fully the price differences which appear to exist.[6]

Evidence on margins is shown in Table 11.3. This table shows net (after tax) price-cost margins in 1994 for a number of leading French and UK supermarket chains. Although the comparison is fairly crude, it shows that margins are also higher in leading UK supermarket groups compared to their counterparts in France.

Table 11.3 Profit margins: net profits after tax (%), 1994

	1994
Carrefour	1.3
Promodès	0.8
Casino	0.8
Sainsbury	5.2
Tesco	4.8
Safeway	4.8

Source: Keynote, 1996.

In this case, again, margins may be higher because of higher land costs and higher costs of building, or because UK supermarket chains invest more in their stores, e.g. by providing a better quality shopping environment than French stores. The evidence seems to suggest, however, that margins in the UK are too high and more competition is required.

11.2.2 Problems for Farmers

Another issue has been the relationship between UK supermarket chains and farmers, and, in particular, whether supermarket chains have been exerting monopsony power against farmers. This has been an issue, in particular, in relation to livestock markets and has led to direct action by farmers against some supermarket chains.[7]

The evidence on this is mixed. In our interviews, one representative of a farming group claimed that supermarket chains exert monopsony power in livestock auctions (e.g. by using the same agent to bid for all of their meat). The supermarket chains deny this and we were able to obtain no corroborative evidence to support it.

It was also suggested to us that the main reason for the drop in livestock prices has been the decline in demand for meat. This is associated independently with the crisis over BSE, the high exchange rate and the long term decline in demand for red meat. Hence, while recognising that marginal farmers have been forced out of business, and prices for farmers remain very low, it was argued that this was primarily due to the fall in demand rather than the actions of the supermarket chains.

These claims are difficult to test without a large scale study. However, in its report, the Competition Commission (2000) concluded that low prices were primarily due to low demand, and we accept this view. The Commission also found that the claim of some farmers that the supermarkets did not pass on the low prices to consumers was not borne out by the evidence, in that margins were typically found to be small and no evidence of profiteering was found.[8]

11.2.3 Fees and Rebates

In our interviews, a number of types of behaviour were identified as possibly involving anti-competitive behaviour. Of course, negotiations between buyers and suppliers can be confrontational and this was clearly recognised. It was suggested, however, that major buyers are able to dictate particularly favourable terms and conditions to suppliers. These include:

- *listing allowances*: payments made to supermarkets to list a new product, and place it on their shelves for a set number of weeks.
- *special promotions*: paid for by producers and typically involving promotion over a two week period at the end of an aisle (called a 'gondola' in the UK).
- *two-for-one (or similar) offers*: these can be suggested by the supermarket chains or their suppliers, and typically involve suppliers having to make discounts on the products involved.
- *over-riders*: these are payments made at the end of the year by suppliers (i.e. rebates), if particular sales targets have been met.
- *drop allowances*: allowances given to suppliers for delivering goods to a central depot. (It was argued that supermarket chains kept some of the benefit of this for themselves.)

These kinds of fees are paid in each of the countries in our sample and it is clearly not necessarily the case that they should be regarded as anti-competitive (although, as we have seen in earlier chapters, over-riders have been viewed with some scepticism in Spain and France). Apart from specific contractual terms, the leading supermarket chains also have significant power over small (including small own brand) suppliers, in negotiating the lowest possible prices.

In its report, the Competition Commission (2000) argued that there was evidence of anti-competitive behaviour arising from this network of practices. Specifically, they found that the five largest firms (Tesco, Sainsbury, Asda, Safeway and Somerfield) had significant market power, and were able to exploit their position to the detriment of suppliers. The Commission identified 52 practices commonly found in the sector of which 27 were found to be against the public interest. These included changes in contractual arrangements at short notice, the use of over-riders and retroactive discounts, contributions to store openings, funding promotions and so on. As a result, the Commission recommended that a Code of Practice should be introduced into the industry to regulate such anti-competitive behaviour, and that this code should allow independent dispute resolution.[9]

11.2.4 Other Issues

The Competition Commission report also considered several other issues. First, it noted that some retail groups sell frequently purchased items below cost. In contrast to the Galland Law in France, however, it argued that it was not clear that intervention would be desirable and no remedies were suggested.[10] Similarly, while it found evidence that some retail groups set different prices in different locations (what it referred to as 'price-flexing' in the report), depending on the strength of local competition in those areas (i.e. they engaged in price discrimination), it again concluded that no remedy was required. Finally, in some local areas (notably, in the South-East) where concentration was quite high, it argued that there was scope for abuse of monopoly power. In this case, it suggested that the Director General of Fair Trading should be given the necessary power to approve new developments by existing firms (e.g. if an existing firm sought to acquire or build a new store in that area).

There is some doubt that these measures will be strong enough, particularly if concentration continues to increase. The queries are straightforward: will smaller suppliers, in particular, be prepared to complain about buying practices of supermarket chains if they supply one hundred per cent of their supplies to one store (or group)? Will the measures designed to stop increased concentration in local markets be strong enough? And how much more concentrated should the market be allowed to become? These are all issues to which we return in the final chapter of the book.

11.3 BUYING GROUPS

With the increase in market concentration over recent years and the increasingly dominant position of the four leading chains of multiples, joining a buying or a symbol group is an important element in the survival of smaller retailers. Table 11.4 shows the turnover of the main buying groups (the first three in the table) and symbol groups (the second three) for 1996. The table also shows the leading four retail chains in order to give an idea of the relative importance of buying groups.

Table 11.4 Buying groups' (and multiples') turnover, 1996

	No. of members	Group turnover (£m)	% of Tesco's turnover
Todays	435	6800	59
Landmark	32	1500	13
Lekkerland	11	270	2
Spar	2400	1300	11
Londis	1415	251	2
Mace	1150	500	4
Tesco		11560	100
Sainsbury		10214	88
Asda		6010	52
Safeway		6060	52

Source: Mintel report on wholesaling and cash and carry, June 1996.

Lekkerland UK is part of Lekkerland Group Europa, and Landmark is a member of BIGS (Buying International Group Spar), Todays is a member of EMD (European Marketing Distribution), and Spar is a member of Spar International; thus, over half of these groups have international affiliations. At the moment, however, most of these groups operate at national level, and the main role of these international linkages is information exchange.

Both buying and symbol groups give their members the advantage of enhanced economies of scale in purchasing. In the case of symbol groups this corporate identity goes beyond this purchasing activity, and extends to marketing support for retailing. In this latter case, members operate under a symbol group facia, and are subject to disciplines as regards unity of style and coherent product offering, although retaining their own financial autonomy. A very recent variant of the symbol group is the development of logo facias, where the traders sign a three-year agreement to purchase a given value of stock in exchange for marketing services and preferential prices on shop fittings and equipment. Buying groups differ from symbol groups because their members operate autonomously and are united only with respect to purchasing activity. Membership of both types of group is relatively fluid and requires firms to satisfy certain requirements of operational performance which vary across the groups consistent with their particular aims.

Although buying groups operate in the UK, they only supply a small (and declining) part of the market. This contrasts sharply with the experience of some other countries (e.g. Spain). In the UK, buying groups are at a disadvantage because they do not buy on such a large scale as major supermarket chains, and because they cannot guarantee location within store. The net result is that they tend to obtain lower discounts than the major retail chains. As the independent retail sector continues to decline, it is anticipated that their importance in the UK will decline still further.

11.4 OWN BRANDS

Own brands have become a major feature of UK food retailing. Their market share, in aggregate, is estimated at 37 per cent in 1996 (Table 11.5), but is much higher for the major multiples as can be seen in Table 11.6.

Table 11.5 Own brand shares of total retail sales (%)

	1990	1991	1992	1993	1994	1995	1996
Own brand share	24.1	25.7	27.8	31.3	32.0	34.1	36.7

Source: Euromonitor, 1998.

Own brands cover a wide range of products, and can be divided into two categories: high quality and low quality products. Own brand products were first introduced with the aim of competing directly with branded products. Their quality level has been improving over the last couple of decades and, at the high end, is now considered very close, if not identical, to the quality level of branded products. This allows them to compete with the latter for consumers located in the upper and medium segment of the market. In supermarkets, they are usually located on shelves very close to the branded products where they are given a generic name (for example, the name of the supermarket) and tend to mimic very closely the packaging and presentation of the branded products.

Low quality own brand products represent a much smaller segment of the market, and their introduction can be linked to the arrival in the UK of discounters who offer products of a lower perceived quality at a lower price.

Their aim and characteristics are therefore different: they are basic products, of lower perceived quality, with basic packaging (with the aim of reducing costs)

Table 11.6 Own brand shares for major retail chains (%), 1994–95

	1994	1995
Sainsbury	66	68
Tesco	56	59
Waitrose	56	57
Safeway	52	57
Somerfield	45	48
Asda	41	43
Coops	41	39
Kwik Save	13	20

Source: Keynote, 1996.

and a name that strongly suggests their competitive approach (e.g. *Tesco Value, Sainsbury Essentials, Safeway Savers*), and they are offered at a very low price, in order to compete in the lowest segment of the market. Table 11.7 shows the proportion of high and low quality own brand products by value in the major supermarkets in 1996.

Table 11.7 Proportion of high and low quality own labels (%), 1996

	HQ	LQ
Tesco	41.0	3.8
Sainsbury	52.4	1.3
Safeway	36.6	3.6

Source: *Marketing Week*, 28th June 1996.

   A breakdown of own brand shares by product category is given in Table 11.8, illustrating the high and increasing penetration levels for many key food items. Overall, the share of own brand products has been steadily increasing in the 1990s (see Table 11.5). An important consequence of this has been the disappearance from supermarkets of secondary brands (selling at less than the leading branded goods in a particular category). For most of their manufacturers the only chance of survival has been to start producing for supermarket own labels. Moreover, in some product areas it is now the case that the only branded product sold by a supermarket chain is the brand leader, so that competition within the supermarket between branded products has lost importance in favour of competition between the brand leader and their own brand products.

Table 11.8 Own label shares by category of product (%)

	1993	1996	Change
Chilled and ambient pizzas	86.2	88.2	2.0
Prepared salads	82.0	88.0	6.0
Frozen and chilled poultry products	74.1	78.5	4.4
Fresh poultry	64.7	75.3	10.6
Frozen poultry	59.8	65.0	5.2
Morning goods	66.9	74.8	7.9
Cheese	66.3	72.3	6.0
Milk	53.6	64.2	10.5
Cream	56.2	63.9	7.7
Frozen vegetables	59.5	59.3	-0.2
White fat & oils	51.3	58.0	6.7
Wrapped bread	47.4	57.9	10.5
Fruit juice	48.9	57.0	8.1
Defined frozen poultry products	46.3	56.5	10.2
Canned fruit	44.2	56.0	11.8
Chilled desserts	48.7	54.0	5.3
Frozen fish	53.7	52.5	-1.2
Cakes & pastries	45.3	52.2	6.9
Wet fish	-	51.2	51.2
Pastes, spreads & pates	36.7	49.8	13.1
Plain & savoury rice and pasta	44.3	49.6	5.3

Source: Super Panel/MAPS, 1997.

As has been suggested for other countries, UK supermarket chains tend to set high margins on own brand products. Examples of this are shown in Table 11.9. In part, this is because the supermarkets use their buying power to obtain very low prices from own brand suppliers. However, supermarkets are much more closely involved in bringing own brand products to market and hence incur costs (e.g. in relation to packaging, marketing, legal matters and logistics) which are not borne on branded goods and this makes comparisons of gross margins difficult. Nevertheless, there seems to be no doubt that UK supermarkets make higher profits on own brands if only because margins on branded goods are often very low.

As the importance of own brands has increased and their role has changed, some brand manufacturers have started producing for own labels. These include

Unilever, Nestlé, PepsiCo, Danone, McCain, Campbell, Allied Lyons and others, including recently Heinz. Not all manufacturers agree to produce own labels, however, and some of them (e.g. Kelloggs, Coca-Cola and Gillette) consider it prejudicial to their (quality) reputation.

Table 11.9 Retailer gross margins (%), 1993

	Own label	Brand leader
Baked beans	18	2
Soft drinks	26	26
Household detergents	20	6
Paper products	26	6
Cigarettes	10	8

Source: *Independent Grocer/PLMA*, 1993.

The relationship between producers of branded goods and retailers has become more complicated since the former have started producing for the latter's own label goods. There is evidence that in some cases production deals can be used as negotiation tools, for example, for the stocking of other branded goods by the same manufacturer, so the relationship is mutually beneficial. However this is not always the case, as evidenced by the growing number of claims and complaints by manufacturers, and by the forming of a special association to protect their rights, the British Brands Group. Apart from unfair competition claims against 'copy-cat' producers, manufacturers have also complained about shelf space and poor in-store product positioning offered by the supermarket chains. Another point about this relationship is that brand producer involvement in the production of own labels entails sharing some cost information with the retailers. The latter can therefore use this information in the negotiation of the price of branded goods.

11.5 PRODUCTS

11.5.1 Washing Powders and Detergents

The share of detergents and other cleaning materials in average consumer expenditure is similar to the share of product groups such as bread, rolls and sweets and higher than the share of the other two products considered in this analysis. This market share has fallen slightly over recent years – see Table 11.10.

Table 11.10 Share of average consumer expenditure on detergents and other cleaning materials

	A	B
1993/94	3.16	0.63
1994/95	3.14	0.62
1996/97	3.07	0.60
Rate of Change 93/94–96/97	-2.83	-4.64

Notes:

A: Average weekly consumer expenditure on product /Average weekly expenditure on food and fast moving consumer goods (%).
B: Average weekly consumer expenditure on product / Total average weekly expenditure (%).

Source: Family Spending, CSO, 1998.

The UK market for washing powders and other detergents can be considered mature and saturated. Laundry detergents are a basic commodity, and, therefore, their value growth depends very much on technological innovations that add value and justify price increases. The limited growth (see Table 11.11) of market sales over the period 1993–97 (up 10.31 per cent in nominal terms) can be explained mainly by two factors: on the one hand, the period has been characterised by fierce price competition between the two brand leaders (Procter & Gamble, and Unilever) and retailer own brands, and, on the other hand, a regression from more expensive concentrated detergents to cheaper standard detergents.

Table 11.11 Sales of washing powders and detergents (£m), 1993–97

	1993	1994	1995	1996	1997
Detergents	805	815	823	849	888

Source: Market Research GB, July 1998.

The market can be considered a virtual duopoly in which Procter & Gamble enjoy a dominant position with 56 per cent of the market in 1997 and Lever Bros (Unilever) has a 28 per cent market share (Table 11.12). The importance of private label products in this sector is limited in the UK context but still significant. In the last five years the biggest supermarket chains have invested in complete washing powder lines (Sainsbury's *Novon*, Safeway's *Cyclon*, Tesco's *Advance* and Asda's *Integra*, all produced by independent Robert McBride) but this has not had a major effect on leading firm sales. This is almost certainly due to the strong brand image of the major products, fostered by heavy advertising, although own brands have increased their share from about nine per cent in 1992 to 15 per cent by 1997.

Table 11.12 Market shares in washing powders and other detergents (%)

		1996	1997
P&G		55.9	56.0
	Ariel	25.1	24.0
	Bold	12.4	14.3
	Daz	11.5	10.3
	Fairy	5.6	6.1
	Dreft	1.3	1.0
Lever Bros.		28.0	27.6
	Persil	21.3	22.0
	Surf	3.9	3.4
	Radion	2.8	2.2
Private Labels		14.3	15.2
Others		1.8	1.2

Source: Mintel, 1998.

As far as buying power is concerned, this is a classic case where major multinational producers face major supermarket chains. Bargaining takes place between the major suppliers and the major supermarket chains and own brands act as a bargaining counter for the supermarket chains.

11.5.2 Coffee

The UK coffee market is distinguished from the market in the other three countries studied in that instant coffee is very much more important than roast and ground coffee in the UK. In 1997, retail sales of instant coffee were £653 million (89 per cent) compared to just £82 million (11 per cent) for roast and ground coffee (Table 11.13). This is almost exactly the reverse of the position in Germany and similarly is different from that in France and Spain. On the other hand, the UK market in roast and ground coffee has been growing faster than instant coffee in recent years (by 55 per cent compared to 25 per cent for instant coffee (in nominal terms) between 1992 and 1997) but, of course, from a much lower base.

The instant coffee sector is dominated by Nestlé with 58 per cent of the market in 1996, followed by Kraft Jacobs Suchard with 22 per cent and own

Table 11.13 Retail sales of instant and roast and ground coffee (£m)

	Instant	R&G	Total
1992	523	53	576
1993	515	52	567
1994	582	59	641
1995	662	79	741
1996	650	81	731
1997	653	82	735

Source: Mintel, 1998.

brands with 16 per cent (Table 11.14). Nestlé's dominance is maintained by strong advertising of its major brands (e.g. Néscafe and Gold Blend) and this has meant that it has apparently been able to resist pressure from supermarket chains to reduce its price. It has been helped by the fact that own brand coffees are perceived as inferior in quality to branded goods, and this has meant that own brand sales are relatively low compared to other grocery items in the UK. Even with improvements in the quality of own brand products in recent years, consumers still perceive them to be inferior, and have tended to continue to buy branded products.

Table 11.14 Market shares in the instant coffee market (%), 1992–96

	1992	1994	1996
Nestlé	54	54	58
Kraft Jacobs Suchard	23	22[1]	22
Own brand	15	17	16
Other brands	8	7	4

Note: [1] includes Allied-Lyons products for 1994.

Source: Mintel, 1998.

There is no dominant producer of roast and ground coffee. Three firms, however, have market shares above ten per cent: Sara Lee (Douwe Egberts) (15 per cent), KJS (14 per cent) and Paulig (13 per cent) (Table 11.15). Of these, Paulig has seen substantial growth in market share since 1992. In this sector, own brands are much more important with 42 per cent of sales in 1996, and this is just above the UK average for own brand sales. The strength of the own brand sector means that supermarket chains may be better placed to extract lower prices from the leading suppliers than from the leading instant coffee producers.

It seems likely that changes in consumer preferences will induce further growth in the roast and ground coffee sector in the next few years, at the expense of instant coffee and tea.

Table 11.15 Market shares in roast and ground coffee (%), 1992–96

	1992	1994	1996
Sara Lee	11	13	15
Kraft Jacobs Suchard	19	16*	14
Paulig	6	21	13
Lyons Tetley	19	-	-
Own Label	38	39	42
Other Brands	8	10	16

Note: * includes Allied-Lyons products for 1994.

Source: Mintel, 1998.

11.5.3 Butter and Margarine

Butter and margarine can be considered as two independent sub-markets. In 1996, joint retail sales in these two sub-markets was £906 million, of which £344 million (38 per cent) corresponded to sales of butter and £562 million (62 per cent) corresponded to sales of margarine.

Table 11.16 The UK market for butter and margarine, 1992–97

	Tonnes	£m at 1992 prices
1992	495	837
1993	486	825
1994	475	810
1995	462	802
1996	459	793
1997	460	794

Source: Mintel, 1998.

Tables 11.16 and 11.17 show the overall evolution of the UK market for butter and margarine and other spreads in the period 1992–97. Over this period the market experienced negative growth in real terms (-5.13 per cent) and in volume (-7.07 per cent) (Table 11.16). The main factors underlying this fall were the reduction in home baking, the increased use of convenience foods, and health related issues. The market for butter was more or less stable (Table 11.17) but the market for margarine and other spreads fell by 8.7 per cent.

Table 11.17 Retail sales of butter, margarine and other spreads (£m at 1992 prices)

	Margarine and other spreads	Butter
1992	540	297
1993	527	298
1994	513	297
1995	506	296
1996	492	301
1997	493	301

Source: Mintel, 1998.

Table 11.18 shows the market shares in margarine and other spreads in 1994 and 1996. Van den Bergh Foods (Unilever) is the leading producer with 43 per cent of the market in 1996, followed by St. Ivel with 25 per cent and Dairy Crest with ten per cent. Own brands make up most of the rest with a share of 19 per cent in 1996. An important feature of this part of the market is the development of new products such as margarines made from sunflower oil, olive oil and so on. While these developments offer scope for new entry, active development of new products by the leading firms has tended to keep new entrants at bay.

Table 11.18 Market shares in margarine and other spreads, 1994 and 1996

Company	1994 (% value)	1996 (% value)
Van de Bergh Foods	42	43
St. Ivel	25	25
Dairy Crest	12	10
Own label	18	19
Others	3	3

Source: Mintel, 1998 and *Own Label*, 1997.

In the butter segment, three brands dominate: Anchor with 35 per cent of the market, Lurpak (MD Foods) with 18 per cent and Country Gold (Dairy Crest) with 11 per cent, while a fourth brand, Kerrygold, has five per cent (Table 11.19). Own label products account for nearly a quarter of the market (24 per cent). In contrast to other countries in our sample (e.g. Spain and Germany) local supply does not appear to be a major factor in the UK. Nevertheless, concentration is only moderate in this sector, and the strength of own brands is such that this market is seen as relatively competitive in the UK. Butter is also

Table 11.19 Market shares in butter, 1994 and 1996

	1994 (%value)	1996 (% value)
Anchor	32	35
Lurpak (MD Foods)	18	18
Country Gold (Dairy Crest)	11	11
Kerrygold	5	5
Own label	23	24
Other	11	7

Source: Mintel, 1998 and *Own Label*, 1997.

one of the products used by supermarket chains to attract customers into their stores, so that margins on branded butter are generally very thin. This benefits the consumer, but (possibly) at the expense of putting pressure on prices of the smaller suppliers.

NOTES

1. Symbol groups are, typically, smaller stores which carry the same name (the most common being the Spar Group) and combine to increase their buyer power *vis-à-vis* suppliers.
2. It is estimated at the time of writing that Tesco's market share has increased to about 20 per cent with further reductions in the share of small independent firms.
3. More recently (1999), Asda has been taken over by the US retailer Wal-Mart.
4. *Sunday Times* (23 August 1998 and 30 August 1998).
5. They did note, however, that the possibility of monopoly pricing was an issue in some local areas where competition was not strong.
6. Interestingly, evidence in the period since the investigation suggests that significantly greater price competition has emerged, in particular from the market leader Tesco. This implies that there was scope for more competition than perhaps the Commission felt.
7. The primary form of action has been picketing of centraldepots of supermarket chains. This took place in particular in 1998 and 1999 in Wales, where farmers attempted to stop deliveries (both in and out of) depots.
8. Meat and some other goods (e.g. butter) are, typically, priced very low in supermarkets as 'almost' loss leaders which attract customers into stores. The supermarket chains therefore do have a very strong incentive to buy such products at the lowest possible price. The evidence, however, appears to be that they don't operate monopsonistically as alleged.
9. The Commission considered using a voluntary code but concluded that this would be insufficient. It is not clear, however, that its proposals would go much beyond a voluntary code in practice.
10. The Commission cites evidence from the Irish Fair Trade Commission which suggests that similar measures led to increased prices and a decrease in competition in Ireland.

12. Issues and Lessons Arising from the Case Studies

12.1 INTRODUCTION

In this part we have examined food retailing in four EU countries: France, Germany, Spain, and the UK, and in three product groups: washing powders and detergents, coffee, and butter and margarine. In all four countries, there have been considerable increases in concentration in food retailing in the last 20 years. In France (and, to some extent, Germany), there has been rapid growth in large hypermarket groups, and these organisations have also moved into other EU markets (such as Spain). In the UK, food retail concentration is the highest of the four countries; the UK has the most developed own label sector and developed emphasis on one-stop shopping and high retail service. Germany is of interest because of the high market shares of discounters, and the effect this has had on competition at the retail stage, and between suppliers and retailers. Spain is an example of a country with more traditional retail outlets and lower concentration, but where concentration is now increasing rapidly and the sector appears to be in a transitional phase.

The three product groups given special attention actually yielded five sub-products for investigation as the coffee market was clearly segmented into roast/ground coffee and instant coffee while fat spreads were divided into butter and non-butter (margarine) spreads. The examination of these five sub-products allowed consideration of a variety of experiences concerning buyer power in the different countries. Initially, the products were selected for the study because they were all major products within the consumer's shopping basket and represent clearly different elements of the basket of regularly purchased items from grocery stores. In the case studies, however, it became clear that for the purposes of analysis these products can also be divided into two categories: products in which relatively few producers face large buyers and engage in bilateral bargaining (washing powders, instant coffee and, in some cases, roast and ground coffee, and margarine) and products where generally competitive suppliers face large buyers (butter, and in some other cases, roast and ground coffee). While, in both categories, similar types of issue arose in terms of buyer power, there was some concern that competitive suppliers might experience greater difficulties than more oligopolistic firms; often they have more at stake than larger firms (because de-listing of their product might well force them out of business).

The studies show that buyer power is a feature of food retailing in all four countries considered, but significant differences exist between them. In the UK, four supermarket chains dominate the market and buying groups are not a major feature. In contrast, in the other countries, buying groups are much more important and account for a significant proportion of sales (see Table 7.10). Second, food retailers in France (and, to a lesser extent, Germany) have been involved in considerable cross-border activity, notably in Spain but also in other countries, including Germany with Intermarché's acquisition of Spar in 1997. German discounters have also been moving into other countries, including France and the UK, while UK food retailers have made some tentative steps to move into other countries (e.g. the recent move of Tesco into Ireland and Poland). Spain is of interest because retail sales have become dominated by French supermarket/hypermarket chains which appear to be able to exert considerable buyer power. In Germany, while significant buyer power exists, this is accompanied by strong competition at the retail level.

In terms of the representativeness of the countries studied, Table 7.4 (Chapter 7) shows that the UK has slightly above average concentration in food retailing (a five-firm concentration ratio of 56 per cent as opposed to the EU average of 53 per cent in 1996), while France has slightly below average concentration (51 per cent), Germany has somewhat lower concentration (45 per cent) and Spain (of the four) has low concentration (28 per cent). Spain is representative of the southern countries in the EU which tend to have lower concentration in food retailing (particularly Greece (28 per cent) and Italy (12 per cent)) while the other three are more typical of the average level of concentration in the EU. However, the studies do not cover any of the very high concentration countries (e.g. Finland and Sweden) where small country size has led to high concentration..

With regard to the three products studied, it is more difficult to say that these or indeed any other three products could be considered representative of all food and other fast moving consumer goods sold by grocery retailers. But the three products selected are all major items in the typical consumer shopping basket and they do cover the different broad categories of product sold by retail chains, representing clearly different elements of the basket of regularly purchased items from grocery stores.

In the next section, we return to the issue of market definition, now using the case studies to illustrate our discussion. Section 12.3 then recalls the framework developed in Chapter 3 and reviews what we have learned from the case studies about the applicability of our framework. The chapter closes in section 12.4 with a specific example of the short-run/long-run trade-off which overlays much of the discussion of the welfare impact of buyer power in general.

12.2 MARKET DEFINITION ISSUES

An important initial step in assessing the existence of market power is to consider the definition of the market. As discussed in section 4.3 above, this involves considering two aspects of the market: its geographic extent and the substitutability of products. In addition, in the buyer power context, two types of market are, typically, involved: the retail market where supermarket chains act as sellers to final consumers and the upstream market where retail chains act as buyers of products for resale downstream. The extent of the market is crucial in each of these dimensions: if it is defined too narrowly then the market power of the major retail players may be overstated, and if it is defined too broadly, market power may be understated.

In food retailing, consumers usually shop locally so that, from their point of view, the market is basically local (sub-regional). However, on a broader view, supermarkets and hypermarkets in each country (although less so for Spain) have penetrated many of these local markets and, given that they typically adopt uniform prices across most markets, it makes sense to view them nationally. In some markets, of course, there are gaps in the chain of substitutes so that changes in prices in some areas do not necessarily have a significant effect elsewhere. For example, it could be the case that in a rural area, there is no supermarket nearby, and, in fact, consumers shop locally in smaller shops. In this kind of case, one could find a break in the chain of substitutes such that the appropriate market for these consumers is (strictly) local. It is also possible that markets can be supra-national where consumers are near to borders (e.g. in the Benelux countries) and so can shop elsewhere if national prices rise. However, partly through lack of data (at the more disaggregated level), we take the pragmatic view that retail markets can be viewed as national in most cases.

In the product sense, markets can be defined where it is possible to identify a gap in the chain of substitutes for a particular good. If we take a product in a particular geographic region, then we can consider the following hypothetical experiment: suppose the price is at the competitive level and the firms in the market (as currently defined) increase prices permanently by 5–10 per cent, what is the effect on their profits? If profits are reduced significantly, then we conclude that the market as defined is too narrow and needs to be widened, but if they are not (and assuming that one starts from a relatively narrow definition), then the level of market aggregation is correct.

In the instant coffee case, for example, the question is: can we regard instant coffee as a market in itself, or should we widen the definition to include roast and ground coffee, other hot beverages (such as tea), other soft drinks, etc.? In the UK, where instant coffee dominates the retail market, an increase in price of 5–10 per cent (from the competitive level) would be likely to have only a limited effect on coffee sales (in our view), hence the market can be defined at this level. In France, Germany and Spain instant coffee is only a small part of the total coffee market but (we would argue) that a similar argument would apply, i.e. that a 5–10 per cent increase in price from the competitive level would have only a relatively small effect on profits from instant coffee sales. In these countries, instant coffee has a niche market but it is still appropriate for it to be seen as a market in itself as substitution to roast and ground coffee (or other beverages) is not likely to be great for such a price rise.

Similar arguments probably apply to the other products in our sample. Instant coffee is, probably, not a close substitute for roast and ground coffee in any of the markets we discuss. In washing powders (in all countries) no close substitutes exist and hence washing powders is likely to be a market on the definition that we use. In the case of butter and margarine (or non-butter spreads), the products are more substitutable, however. In a given geographic region, a 5–10 per cent rise in, say, butter prices from competitive levels may have a significant effect on the profits of butter producers, and one might therefore consider these goods as one product as far as defining the retail market is concerned. At the very least, therefore, one would want to look at this issue in defining the market, given also that it might make a significant difference in determining market power in the market (in particular) for margarine.

A similar type of approach can be adopted in considering the market upstream. In this case, a market can be defined in terms of the effect of a reduction of 5–10 per cent in the price paid to suppliers; if this causes suppliers to refuse to supply goods which, in turn, limits the range of goods that supermarkets can offer, then supermarket profits will be reduced and the market definition would be too narrow. On the other hand, if the supermarkets can introduce such price reductions and suppliers are forced to comply with them, then the market will be defined at this particular level.

Clearly, markets may not be defined at this level in the same way as at the retail level. As far as the geographical extent of the market is concerned, supermarket chains typically buy at the national level although in some cases (e.g. for fresh vegetables and butter – see below) they may buy more locally, and, in others, they may buy internationally. If we consider an example (washing powders), suppliers of washing powders may be forced to accept a 5–10 per cent cut in price if implemented by a hypothetical monopsonist in a country since to refuse to supply at that level would be very costly for them indeed. Yet at a regional level, the price cut is likely to be resisted. If this is the case, then it makes sense to view the market as national rather than regional since at the latter level suppliers would be much more likely to play regions off against each other. If, however, suppliers of washing powders are big and powerful in many countries in Europe (or more widely) then they may be prepared to refuse to supply supermarkets if faced with a 5–10 per cent price cut even at national level, in which case the market may be seen as supra-national. In our view, this market is more readily seen as national rather than supra-national because even the large producers (Unilever, Procter & Gamble, etc.) would probably have too much to lose at national level.

A similar analysis can be applied to instant coffee, roast and ground coffee and margarine. In the case of butter, particularly in Spain and Germany where butter is typically sourced from local (or regional) suppliers, the definition of the market is more likely to be at the local (or regional) rather than national level. In these cases, suppliers at the local/regional level may not be able to resist a 5–10 per cent cut in price and hence the appropriate market definition will be at the regional level.

On the product side, the issue centres on whether a hypothetical monopsonist in a given geographic area can reduce price for a product by 5–10 per cent such that suppliers can (or cannot) refuse to supply. For a narrowly defined product (e.g. tuna in olive oil), suppliers will be more likely to be able to resist such a price cut and hence the market will be defined too narrowly. If the hypothetical retail monopsonist tried to reduce price by this amount for all canned fish in a given geographic region, it may be less easy for suppliers to resist and hence the market will be defined at this level. In the case of coffee, for example, in a particular country, although producers may produce both instant, and roast and ground coffee, it is likely that a hypothetical reduction in price of, say, roast and ground coffee by 5–10 per cent, would not induce sufficient refusal to supply to make this change unprofitable, and hence roast and ground coffee would be a suitable market definition.

12.3 GENERAL APPLICATION OF THE BUYER POWER FRAMEWORK

With the above comments on market definition in mind, we now turn our attention to the specific issue of buyer power and the findings from the case studies using the framework set out in Chapter 3 above. Our purpose here is to draw on the case studies to illustrate the applicability of the framework – to ask, is it a potentially helpful tool to the policy maker?

The framework represented by Table 3.1 poses five questions that should be considered in analysing buyer power. We consider each of these in turn from a general perspective, but bearing in mind that the application of the framework is intended to address specific cases of alleged abuse of buyer power. In practice, it is clear that in some cases buyer power provides economic benefits (e.g. where it leads to countervailing power to that of oligopolistic suppliers which reduces prices to the final consumer). In other cases, however, buyer power can lead to possible policy concern (e.g. where retailers impose unfair terms and conditions on suppliers or where retailers create dependency relationships with small suppliers which may adversely affect supplier viability/efficiency or distort competition at the retail or producer level).

12.3.1 Is there Significant Buyer Power?

This is, of course, the key preliminary question and without it there is no reason to proceed with an investigation. Two factors are identified as providing evidence for this: significant proportions of the product as a whole purchased by a firm and significant arrangements of terms of purchase (such as listing fees) by a firm.

Our case studies indicate that large buyers do have this power in each country studied, whether in the form of retail chains or buyer groups where their size and market share allow them to extract more favourable terms from suppliers compared to those obtained by small independent/unaffiliated retailers. Bulk buying economies of the large groups are a key factor accounting for the advantageous terms they receive. But additional benefits can be derived from the strong strategic position held by large retail/buyer groups, where they can credibly play off suppliers against each other when offering contracts (say, for supplying an own-label product line) or credibly use a threat of de-listing even against significant brand producers.

Such buyer power might generally be found in most EU member states where large buyers dominate market purchases. However, it is less certain that this applies in countries such as Italy and Greece where buyer concentration is very low and where traditional food retailing continues to predominate. Yet even here the indications are that retailer concentration will increase substantially in the next few years and similar issues of buyer power may then arise as well.

The five firm buyer concentration measure gives an indication of the extent to which suppliers are likely to be dependent on the major buyers in each country. From Table 7.10, for the UK, where buyer groups are not significant, the largest five retail groups accounted for 56 per cent of food distribution in 1996. In the other three countries, the presence of large buyer groups raises buyer concentration significantly above the corresponding retail concentration level such that in France the largest five buyers accounted for 78 per cent of food purchases in 1996, while the figures for Germany and Spain were 50 per cent and 49 per cent, respectively.

In practice, though, individual suppliers will be more dependent for their sales than indicated by these levels, given that unless they produce 'must-stock' brands which all retailers will wish to take, their sales will be concentrated on particular key buyers. Our survey highlighted the extent of this dependency for suppliers in each of the three product groups considered. For instance, an own label supplier made all its UK sales to the top four retail chains. A leading branded goods producer estimated that 75 per cent of its sales in Germany went to its top five customers (four leading retail chains and a leading buying group) and that this had increased from 33 per cent in 1988. In Spain, the importance of the buying groups is apparent. For example, one major supplier had 45 per cent of its sales to the five largest retail chains, but its major customers were the two leading buying groups accounting for (a further) 50 per cent of its sales, while for another leading supplier its respective figures were 47 per cent and 39 per cent (i.e. 86 per cent of sales went to its seven largest buyers).

Apart from the ability to extract (per unit) price discounts from suppliers, major buyers also appear well placed to obtain other favourable terms in the form of the up-front fees and other financial benefits they can command from suppliers, principally in the form of listing fees, payments for special promotions, over-riders, drop allowances and so on – see the country chapters for further details. The majority of these allowances involve fees paid to retail/buyer groups for services rendered and they are typical in all four countries, but the forms vary in significance. Thus, for instance, suppliers of a new product commonly pay a major retail chain a listing fee to take a new product and stock it for a set number of weeks. Suppliers normally pay a fee for taking an end-of-aisle display associated with a promotion. And retail chains may link discounts they require to the year's value of sales, requiring suppliers to pay a rebate at the end of the year if certain sales targets have been met.

Some of these practices may be seen as part of 'normal business' which offers advantages to the supplier, for example the extra sales that can be generated through end-of-aisle displays.[1] While such fees allow retailers to increase their profits, and they are clearly exploiting their positions as leading buyers, the potential gains to suppliers mean that from a business perspective, it may seem reasonable to pay for access to the retailer-

controlled scarce resource (i.e. display or shelf space).[2] Other practices
appear more directly detrimental to suppliers, where little is offered in return
for a payment to the retailers. In Spain, for example, it seems to be quite
common for suppliers to be asked to make a payment when a new store is
opened, or on the anniversary of an existing store or something similar. In
addition, in other countries, suppliers are sometimes expected to make
retrospective payments at the end of a year even though these may not be
part of the order agreed.

12.3.2 Is Buying Power against Relatively Powerless Suppliers?

Two factors are relevant in answering this question: absence of evidence that
suppliers dictate terms of sale and low seller concentration in the upstream
market.

Clearly, in any supermarket, a range of products (such as fresh produce
and certain canned goods, etc.) will be produced by relatively atomistic
suppliers, as will many own brand goods. In such markets, strong buyers will
attempt to obtain the lowest possible prices from suppliers by 'squeezing' as
much profit as possible out of them. Moreover, retailers may, potentially,
engage in anti-competitive practices (such as ex post rebates, or demand for
payments to support special store events), which a small supplier may be
forced to pay rather than risk being delisted.

It is evident that oligopolistic competition characterises the suppliers'
market for several of the products considered in our case studies, where
supplier concentration was relatively high, for some countries. However, two
of our sub-products better approximate the case of competitive supply:
butter, and (in part) roast and ground coffee. Butter is supplied competitively
in three of the four countries, where the UK is an important exception as the
four leading brands/producers (Anchor, MD Foods (Lurpak), Country Gold
(Dairy Crest) and Kerrygold) accounted for 69 per cent of sales in 1996. The
supply of roast and ground coffee is competitive in two countries: Spain and
the UK (although, in the latter case, roast and ground coffee has a much
smaller market share than instant coffee), and appears less competitive in the
other two, France and Germany: the largest two firms (KJS and Douwe
Egberts) have a combined market share of 60 per cent in France, and the
largest two firms in Germany (KJS and Tchibo/Eduscho) have a combined
share of 58 per cent.

Our investigation suggests that margins for competitive suppliers of
butter and roast and ground coffee are squeezed by the large retail chains. In
the UK, for example, it appears that many own brand producers operate on
very thin margins, and that retail grocery chains are always keen to pressure
suppliers to lower prices further. This also seems to be the case in France, for

butter, where the risk of being delisted might make suppliers reluctant to complain.

Whether these situations amount to the exploitation of monopsony (or, more strictly, oligopsony) power, in the traditional sense (see Chapter 2) is not immediately obvious, given that it is not clear whether supply is less than infinitely elastic (i.e. the long run supply curve slopes up). Agricultural markets, such as livestock markets, may be examples where farmers can conceivably earn intra-marginal rents given that increasing output may cause prices to rise (and vice versa). But for many grocery items, long run supply curves might typically be horizontal. In the case of coffee, for instance, prices are likely to be determined primarily by the world price of coffee and it seems unlikely that there would be major differences in costs between producers of roast and ground coffee. The case of butter is more speculative, where the localised supply of producers might vary due to differing farming costs, giving rise to the possibility that supply curves might be upward sloping.

For the other products under our consideration, seller concentration is relatively high, notably for washing powders and instant coffee. The issue here is about the share of economic surplus (profits) between the trading parties, generally determined through bargaining (though recognising that agreements may affect the total level of surplus available), rather than supplier viability detrimentally affected by the exploitation of monopsony power. In these markets, where oligopoly characterises both producer and retailer competition, the leading suppliers appear better able to resist retailer pressure to reduce prices and to pay other fees and rebates. In contrast, smaller producers, producing either secondary brands or own labels, are less able to resist such pressure and transfer prices appear much closer to competitive levels.

12.3.3 Does the Buyer Itself have Significant Selling Power?

From the discussion in Chapters 2 and 3, if selling power is present in the downstream market, buyer power may be a means of strategically enhancing it, with potentially adverse welfare effects. If, on the other hand, the final market is generally competitive, buying power is more likely to be socially desirable where the benefits of reduced costs from lower intermediate prices are passed on to consumers by lower retail prices being set.

As in the case of upstream market power, one can use the five firm seller concentration ratio as a structural measure of market power in the retail market, as reported in Table 7.4. In these terms, the UK has the highest concentration ratio (at 56 per cent) of the four countries considered, followed by France (51 per cent), Germany (45 per cent) and Spain (32 per cent).

These figures mask some important differences between the different countries, however. Spain is relatively unconcentrated although the top three firms have market shares between 6 per cent and 10 per cent (Tables 7.6 and 10.2). Germany and France are classified as symmetric oligopolies in Table 7.6 with each of the five leading firms having a market share in a narrow band between 9.4 per cent and 11.9 per cent in France and 6.7 per cent and 10.9 per cent in Germany. In the UK, however, two firms dominate the market with shares of 18.5 per cent and 14.2 per cent respectively, but with two second tier firms with market shares of 9.7 per cent and 9.3 per cent respectively.

In the UK, in particular, there has been public concern that the leading retail chains have been abusing their market power to set high prices and earn high profits. On average, prices tend to be higher in the UK than in other EU countries, notably Germany. While some of this difference is probably due to the strength of sterling, it seems likely on the basis of the evidence discussed in Chapters 9 and 11, that competition is stronger in Germany than the UK. This suggests a cautionary note about using concentration ratios to indicate the presence and abuse of market power since structural measures may not on their own show the true extent of competition.

For Germany, although concentration is quite high, the market appears very competitive. The main engine of this competitiveness is undoubtedly the hard discounters (such as Aldi and Lidl) which accounted for 22 per cent of food retail sales in Germany in 1997, and operate with very low margins. These chains compete on price, inducing other leading chains such as Rewe and Metro to compete on prices as well. In contrast, discounters are much less significant in the UK, where the leading retailers have emphasised retail service provision, with the result that price competition has appeared more relaxed (though it has shown signs recently of intensifying).

Moreover, the intensity of rivalry at the retail stage may have implications for the total share of surplus available between the two levels and result in pressure for suppliers to cut costs and accept lower margins. It was reported to us by some interviewees that negotiations between suppliers and retailers are more relaxed in the UK than say in France or Germany, and that negotiations generally lead to 'satisfactory profits' being earned on both sides. In Germany, however, the reverse is true, and competition at the retail stage appears in turn to lead to greater pressure on suppliers to cut prices (and thus reduce their profits).

12.3.4 Are there Significant Efficiency Gains Associated with Buyer Power? If so, this can be argued in mitigation of buyer concentration.

The case studies show quite clearly that there are significant economies of scale associated with handling large orders. All the suppliers interviewed accepted that there were significant logistic and handling economies associated with selling in bulk, and they all offered discounts to customers to take account of this. The food industry (like many other industries) now uses complex technical modelling to determine the logistics of supply, and to make arrangements with the aim of minimising handling costs, and delivering in bulk is a key factor in this.

Several producers commented, however, that multinational retail chains were increasingly aggregating orders across European countries in order to qualify for a bulk discount, even though there was no logistical advantage at all. These producers try to resist such bulk discount requests, although we were told of one case where a supplier was delisted until it agreed to pay the extra European-wide discount. This is likely to be an increasing feature in the industry as cross-border retailing, and international buying groups, gain strength.

Although cost savings are associated with bulk orders, many suppliers would argue that large retailer and buying groups also try to use their buying power to extract further discounts which are not related to cost savings, and it is clearly these discounts which are a possible cause for concern.

12.3.5 Does the Buyer Attempt to Constrain its Suppliers' Other Actions or Deliberately Create a Dependency Relationship?

If this is so, the arrangement should be treated with suspicion. Examples of this might be exclusive supply arrangements, specific custom designs or arrangements, idiosyncratic specifications or charging structures not obviously related to costs or the goods specified, etc.

As discussed above, it appears quite common for the major groups to command listing fees, special promotions payments, over-riders, drop allowances, and the like. The majority of these payments involve fees paid to retail chains for services rendered. If these practices serve to raise costs for producers, these might be generally passed on to all retailers in the form of higher intermediate (unit) prices, with the effect, in particular, of raising the costs of smaller retailers (who are not in a position to command such allowances), potentially distorting retail competition. In this case, price competition might be dampened, serving to raise retail prices. If so, the practices may be anti-competitive.

In some cases, fees are simply transfers from large suppliers to large supermarket chains, and while suppliers may object to them, they may have little effect on overall social welfare. In fact, if these fees have no other effects, a standard welfare analysis would say they are neutral. In the case of small suppliers, however, large supermarket chains are at a considerable advantage in dealing with smaller firms, and this may lead to an abuse of a dominant position. A number of small firms we contacted told us that the supermarket chains use their market position to drive down prices and to impose additional fees and charges. This is an area of some concern, therefore, where some policy action may be required.

12.4 TRADE-OFFS BETWEEN SHORT-RUN AND LONG-RUN EFFECTS

The interviews conducted for the case studies raised a number of issues. In several places in the book, we have suggested that there is the potential for a classic trade-off between the short and the long run. While increasing buyer power may have immediately welfare-enhancing effects in countering producer power and lowering intermediate prices, in the long run welfare could be harmed if choice is reduced and seller power in retail markets is increased. We close this chapter by pointing to one specific example which has emerged from the case studies.

A common concern raised by producers and representatives of small retailers was that large retailers often appear to sell key branded goods at a loss (as 'loss-leaders'). The practice was regarded as more of an issue of retailer power in general and large retailer pricing tactics, than buyer power specifically. But these may be connected given that producers may have little credible threat of withdrawing supplies to discourage such behaviour given the significant detrimental impact this would have on their profits. The practice can, of course, have direct impact on smaller retailers who are not able to compete at all on such goods. In these instances, there is the suspicion of predatory motives, though the counter-argument is that it is merely a promotional exercise as part of a 'high-low' pricing strategy (as opposed to 'every-day-low-pricing' usually adopted by discounters) to increase total sales levels for the retailer.

The latter point notwithstanding, selling goods below cost by retail chains demands slightly more attention. In this case, because major retail chains sell a range of goods, they have freedom to set individual prices below cost if they so choose. This often means that well-known branded goods are sold at a low price (which may be below cost) and that the chain attempts to recover its costs by charging higher prices on other goods. Such a policy clearly may damage rival firms who sell a more restricted range of goods. From the point of view of having a 'level playing field', therefore, such a practice could well be distortionary and hence undesirable from a welfare point of view – even though some consumers will clearly benefit from the policy, at least in the short run.

The concerns of branded goods producers are mainly on different grounds. For them, their prime concern is that brand investment may be undermined by such activity, if it encourages consumers to perceive their products as low quality, thus adversely affecting their intellectual property rights and discouraging them from investing in building brands. The implications are long term in nature, but how they develop remains to be seen.

NOTES

1. One supplier interviewed reported that a two week end-of-aisle promotion by a retailer led to a 26 fold increase in sales; a demand which they were only just able to meet.
2. The argument is essentially over property rights. With the growth of large supermarket chains, a market has been created in shelf space and end-of-aisle displays where the supermarkets have the property rights. Nevertheless, because the retail chains themselves have market power in these markets, they are likely to earn a higher rent than in a more competitive market.

13. Summary and Conclusions

13.1 INTRODUCTION

Our book has been structured in a straightforward linear fashion, running through economic theory to measurement and policy issues, before confronting the empirical evidence. The evidence is investigated in two complementary ways – statistical analysis of the overall picture, followed by more detailed case studies on some individual member states and products. What does the analysis tell us?

At the heart of this work are the 'buyer power propositions' in Chapter 3. We suggest that these provide a useful checklist when competition policy makers confront specific 'real world' examples of potential concern. Similarly, in terms of the present work, they also provide an obvious framework and identify some of the key concepts and perspectives to be pursued in the subsequent chapters. Some of these perspectives are very familiar within the broader competition policy debate and might be seen as following directly from intelligent application of standard approaches. Perhaps most important, the propositions confirm that a simple-minded blanket policy approach to buyer power, in retailing or elsewhere, would be ill-advised since specific cases will often involve evaluating a trade-off between efficiency and the abuse of market dominance.

However, in other respects, the analysis of buyer power within food retailing raises a set of more specific and perhaps more crucial issues. Consider, for example, concentration and the market shares of leading firms. Given the special nature of the retail market, it is essential to distinguish three aspects of concentration – information on buyer concentration alone is quite insufficient. So far as the exchange of products between manufacturer and retail buyer is concerned, we are interested in the distributions of both producers and retailers. These will affect the price and conditions of exchange and thus the division of rents between the two sets of firms. Yet the relative bargaining strengths of the two sets of firms may be largely irrelevant to final consumers if the retailers, in turn, have no market power in the final distribution market. In other words, an overall assessment of social welfare must be based on an assessment of producer, buyer and (final) seller concentration.

In what follows, we begin by summarising our main conclusions on the structure of EU food retailing and manufacturing. Section 13.3 then considers buyer power and the role of competition policy in this area. Finally, Section 3.4 concludes.

13.2 THE STRUCTURE OF EU FOOD RETAILING AND MANUFACTURING

We begin by summarising our main findings on the structure of the food retailing sector. Traditionally, academic economists have devoted far less attention to retailing than to manufacturing. This means that most of the available evidence on the structure of retailing to date has been produced by firms of consultants or industry experts. Whatever the relative merits of their studies *per se*, they lack the generality, consistency and careful attention to measurement detail that is more typically the hallmark of academics or governmental statistical agencies. One major purpose of this project has been to step back from the numerous and competing sources of information, in order to reconstruct a consistent and integrated overview of the structure of EU food retailing as a whole, as well as that of the individual member states, and the leading firms therein. This has yielded the following six 'headline' facts.

- Aggregate EU retail food seller concentration is high by comparison with manufacturing industry generally. The twenty largest firms account for 40 per cent of aggregate EU retail food turnover, the analogous figure for EU manufacturing being much lower, at 14.5 per cent. Also, in contrast to the general tendency in manufacturing, aggregate EU retail food concentration is rising – by over four percentage points between 1993 and 1996. The leading French and German operators (and, to a lesser extent, UK firms) dominate in the overall statistics. If we take the step, useful for some purposes but misleading for others, of including buyer groups as single entities, retail buyer concentration is even higher than retail seller concentration.
- Retail seller concentration within member states is also high and rising. The average five firm seller concentration ratio in member states rose from 41 per cent in 1993 to 44 per cent in 1996. However, as we document more fully below, there are important and interesting differences between countries.

- With the notable exception of the UK, buyer concentration is even higher – on average, by about ten percentage points – than seller concentration.
- Cross-border operations are expanding rapidly. Of course, 'globalisation', to use a portmanteau term, is not peculiar to this sector, but some features of food retailing are particularly interesting in this respect. As yet, we do not see US (other than the limited entry of Wal-Mart into the German and UK markets) and still less Japanese or Korean multinationals moving into the area. At present, it is mainly just German and French firms which are involved in these activities. Two broad types of development may be identified: (i) movement by the very largest French or German firms into their neighbouring Community countries (Austria, Spain, Portugal, and to some extent Italy); (ii) more pervasive and dispersed expansion by discounters (notably Aldi and Lidl) – rarely occupying the top three or four places in any one nation, but moving broadly into a range of countries. We may speculate that this relates to exploitation of the specific assets developed by these discounters together with the desire to escape from the constraints on growth in the home country.
- This leads us into the key role of the discounters as a force for intense competition, particularly in Germany. We see an important potential force for changes in the market generally arising out of this experience. There is a strong contrast between Germany and the UK, for in the latter country the market leaders have been able to hold on to their dominant position through segmentation of the market within the store. More broadly, discounters are among the rapidly growing retail formats. Although they are rarely the market leaders, they are nevertheless very influential (as we see in the case studies on Germany and France particularly).
- Another feature which seems to be accelerating within food retailing in the Community is mergers between operators. We see these as being of three different types: (i) as a means of new cross-border entry for multinational firms (MNEs) – this carries no obvious immediate market power connotations, but merely changed ownership, (ii) within-country acquisitions by leaders of medium sized competitors – creating an increasing mass in the upper tail of the size distribution at the expense of the middle part of the distribution, (iii) more rarely, mergers among the leaders – notably Kesko/Tuko in Finland and Rewe's acquisition of Meinl in Austria. The EC has rightly become interested in both of the latter two cases.

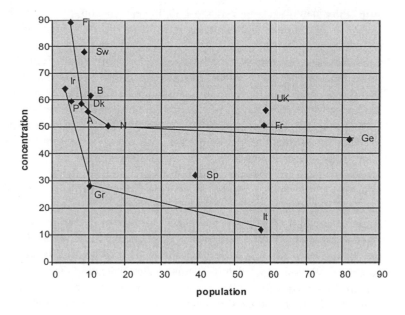

Figure 13.1   Concentration in European food retailing

There is also a seventh observation – probably more accurately referred to as a 'stylised fact' – which we detect from the statistical analysis of Part II:

- Currently, there is a dual structure apparent in food retailing within member states. Figure 13.1 has been constructed by combining information from Table 6.1 and Table 7.4 to depict the relationship between concentration and market size. (Admittedly, these focus on seller concentration, but this appears, from Part II above, to underpin the lower bound to buyer concentration in the market.) The more developed markets, to us, demonstrate a different technology from the undeveloped. The lower bound curve of the developed markets can be seen as described by the points representing Finland, Denmark, Austria, the Netherlands and Germany, but with each of Sweden, Belgium, France and the UK having concentration above that line. Another lower bound is described by Ireland, Greece and Italy, with Portugal slightly above and Spain in an intermediate position.

Turning to the manufacturing sector, we wish to add two further 'headline facts'.

- Producer concentration in the typical food manufacturing industry is fairly high: on average, the five firm concentration ratio, for 3-digit industries at the EU level, is 30 per cent, which is four percentage points higher than the average for all manufacturing industries.
- The importance of the world's largest food MNEs is increasing: this is tabulated statistically in Part II, and notable examples arise in the case studies on coffee and margarine in Part III.

13.3 BUYER POWER AND COMPETITION ISSUES

This book has raised a number of buying power and competition issues in the food retailing sector of the EU. In some cases, policy concerns have been relatively minor (in our view), while in others concerns have been more significant, or we have not been able to obtain sufficient evidence to decide how significant they are. In this section, we focus on the policy issues arising and possible proposals for reform. In what follows, we discuss one broadly positive point (the extent to which consumers gain from the growth of supermarket chains (although there are also producer losses)), and two more negative points (the problem of dependencies, and anti-competitive behaviour of the supermarket chains).

13.3.1 Gains to Consumers (and Producer Losses)

The evidence in the case studies suggests that consumers have benefited from the buyer power of large supermarket chains and from the reduced costs of buying in bulk. In the UK, for example, there has been an overall decline in the real price of food of 9.4 per cent in the period 1989–98[1] and similar declines have no doubt occurred elsewhere. In addition, consumers have benefited from a greater choice of products with many supermarket chains stocking 20,000 or more individual products. Against this, some consumers are worse off due to the closure of smaller stores, and the consequent increase in prices this has induced. This has affected older consumer age groups, in particular, who are unable (or unwilling) to shop in larger supermarket stores (e.g. because of the lack of adequate transport to get to those stores).

In so far as buying power is concerned, producers have generally lost out. Supermarket chains have used their buying power to pressure suppliers to reduce their prices, and given their position in the retail market in many EU countries, suppliers may be forced to accede. In our view, this use of buying power can be seen as undesirable for smaller suppliers (see below), but is less likely to be so for large, often multinational, firms. In this latter case, suppliers are able to use their market power to set high prices in the absence of supermarket groups and supermarket groups can, effectively, use their countervailing buying power to offset this effect. In principle, such action could reduce consumer welfare if it leads to successive mark-ups in the supply and retail chain, or have a neutral effect if suppliers and retailers share monopoly profits. As long as competition is strong at the retail stage, however, supermarket chains will pass on cost reductions to consumers and there is likely to be an overall welfare gain.

The evidence in Part III suggests that in the case study countries (especially Germany and France), price discounts are passed on to consumers, thereby increasing net welfare, and the washing powders market is a good example of this. In the case of the UK, however, there appears to be less pressure on suppliers (at least in this example), and prices may, therefore, be higher than in some EU countries. Nevertheless, substantial price cuts have been passed on to consumers and hence consumer, and net welfare, are likely to have increased.

13.3.2 Economic Dependencies

Our findings suggest that there may be cause for concern where smaller suppliers are concerned. Given that small suppliers may sell most (or all) of their output to a single supermarket chain (or small group of stores), a dependency relation is likely to exist between the supplier and the supermarket chain which supermarket chains may seek to exploit. In our interviews, we found that small suppliers are particularly worried about this, although because of the dependency relation, they were unwilling to allow us to identify them. Standard problems arose from supermarket chains requiring them to make arbitrary payments (e.g. to support a new store opening, to pay an end-of-year rebate, and so on). Small suppliers felt they had to pay these (in their view) unwarranted fees or risk de-listing from the supermarket store or chain, and argued that these payments should not be allowed. In addition, they argued that supermarket chains put too much pressure on them to reduce their prices each year so that they are forced into a situation of not being able to make an adequate return on their investment.

This is clearly worrying and raises the issue of whether it is desirable to introduce a code of conduct (as proposed in the UK) to deal with this issue. As noted in Chapter 11, however, small suppliers are reluctant to make complaints (in case they are identified and de-listed) and this makes for a significant problem even with such a code. In some cases, though, a group of suppliers might be able to make a complaint together (anonymously). Moreover, if a supermarket chain was also shown to be using a practice that was proscribed (see below), it might be more at risk and this could induce it not to use this practice in the first place. Still it is a difficult issue and it is unclear how it can be dealt with effectively.[2]

13.3.3 Anti-Competitive Behaviour

Finally, in the case of anti-competitive behaviour, a number of countries have adopted measures to protect suppliers and, for brevity, we consider the UK case here. In its report, the UK Competition Commission identified 52 practices most of which were carried out by at least one of the leading supermarket chains, of which 27 were found to be against the public interest. These practices included 'requiring or requesting from some of their suppliers various non-cost-related payments or discounts, sometimes retrospectively; imposing charges and making changes to contractual arrangements without adequate notice; and unreasonably transferring risks from the main party to the supplier' (Competition Commission, 2000, vol. 1: Summary and Conclusions, p. 6). Arguably, some of these practices can be seen as transfers in a strict welfare sense, but they can also be seen as anti-competitive in a broader 'fairness' sense. In so far as their effect is judged to be neutral, moreover, there is no economic reason why they should not be proscribed. It would, therefore, seem reasonable to prohibit at least some of these practices.

In the UK it is proposed that a code of conduct be introduced which leading retailers would be required (and other supermarket chains invited) to sign. While this code of conduct is not voluntary (and includes provisions for independent dispute resolution), there are concerns that it will not be tough enough. Hence, depending on circumstances, it might be desirable to prohibit certain practices (in the UK under the Competition Act). If this were done, supermarket chains could be fined heavily if such practices were uncovered, and this would presumably ensure that such practices would be dropped.

13.4 CONCLUSIONS

The analysis in this book suggests that there are some areas of concern over supermarket buying power; most notably, in relation to dependencies of small suppliers and the use of anti-competitive buying practices. On the other hand, supermarket groups have clearly created benefits for consumers (in most countries) bringing lower prices and greater product choice.

The analysis in Chapter 7 shows that five firm concentration is above 50 per cent in most EU countries (the exceptions in 1996 are Germany (45 per cent), Greece (28 per cent), Italy (12 per cent) and Spain (32 per cent): see Table 7.4) and leading firms on average have market shares of 19 per cent (see Table 7.6). Moreover, concentration continues to increase in many countries, and this suggests that it could be an increasing problem. Of course, it is difficult to predict the future and it is possible that cross-national entry (already a developing trend) could reduce concentration rather than that it increase. Nevertheless, as in recent suggestions of mergers in other industries,[3] it could be of significant concern if large concentration-increasing mergers were to take place, and our final conclusion is that competition authorities need to examine such proposed mergers carefully both at national and EU level.

NOTES

1. Competition Commission (2000), vol. 1, Summary and Conclusions, p. 3.
2. As noted in Chapter 9, in its Act on Restraints on Competition which took effect in January 1999, the German Government allows suppliers to make complaints about abuse of purchasing power by a retail chain to remain anonymous in a Cartel Office investigation (although not before the Court). It seems, however, that this on its own would be unlikely to persuade smaller suppliers to come forward.
3. At the time of writing, it has been suggested (by British Airways) that it would be desirable to reduce the number of major airlines operating in Europe to three. At first sight, any proposed mergers to bring this about should be heavily scrutinised before they are allowed (or not allowed) to pass.

Appendix: Questionnaires and Interviews

This appendix outlines the methodology used in the interviews and questionnaires for the case studies in Part III. As noted in the text, interviews were sought for a sample of organisations in order to identify the key issues as perceived by the different market participants in each country. The interviewees were divided into four types: major (and other) retailers in each of the countries concerned, suppliers of the products selected for detailed analysis, buying groups and other interested parties (e.g. trade associations, competition authorities, etc.). Several interviews were also conducted at European head office level (in the case of producers) in relation to the selected products in all four countries.

The interviews at the country level were undertaken by the individual researchers we commissioned to report on each country. Each researcher was asked to identify the major firms and other organisations under the four headings noted above, and to select a number under each heading for interview. They were then asked to contact the organisations to identify contact names. This was followed by a standard letter requesting an interview from the person involved, followed up by a telephone call several days later to make contact with that person. At this stage, the person involved often asked to see the questionnaire to be used and then the appropriate one (from three different questionnaires used depending on whether the respondent was a retailer, a buying group or a producer) was sent to him/her. This was followed up with a further telephone call to arrange a time for interview. Interviews took place over the telephone (the most frequent type) or face-to-face, or, in a few cases, a completed questionnaire was sent back or written material was sent.

In the survey, we were particularly concerned that the views of retailers (as well as producers and others) should be represented. However, responses from retailers in some countries proved difficult to obtain, although we did make special efforts to do this. In the event, we received responses from supermarket chains in three countries but we were unable to do so for Spain (despite the use of a follow-up letter in the latter part of the study). For this reason, we are more cautious over the results in the Spanish case.

The results of the exercise are summarised in Table A.1. Although the aim was not to contact all the key organisations, we did, in fact, contact a large number of them. In all, 118 contacts were made and we were able to obtain 47 interviews/questionnaires returned (i.e. a 40 per cent response rate).

Typical reasons for non-response were that firms did not give interviews or did not want to participate, problems in contacting the people involved and promises of return of the questionnaire which were not fulfilled.

Table A.1 Interviews/questionnaires by country and type of contact

Type of Contact	France	Germany	Spain	UK	European Head Office[4]	Total
Hypermarket/ Supermarket Chains	2	4	-	3	-	9
Producers[1]	5 (1W/2 C/1B)	8 (1W/3C/4 B)	7 (2W/3 B/2C)	1 (1W)	3 (2W/1C)	24
Buying Groups[2]	1	-	-	2	-	3
Other[3]	3	3	1	4	-	11
Total	11	15	8	10	3	47

Notes:
[1] The figures in brackets are for washing powders (W), coffee (C) and butter (B).
[2] Includes four interviews with one buying group for France.
[3] Includes interviews with producer organisations which also dealt with individual products.
[4] These interviews dealt with all four countries.

As shown in the table, responses were obtained from nine supermarket/hypermarket chains, 24 producers, three buying groups and 11 others (including several trade associations and retail groups). While the sample is not large, it should be remembered that this exercise was not undertaken as a full scale survey, but as a way of informing our deskwork analysis in each case. In these terms, the interviews/questionnaires were useful in providing relevant information on the key issues in each of the four countries.

References

AIM (1995), 'Changing Patterns of Retailing and Influence Exercised by Major Retailers', unpublished report, Brussels.

Blair, R.D. and J.L. Harrison (1992), 'The measurement of monopsony power', *Antitrust Bulletin*, **133**, 133-50.

Blair, R.D. and J.L. Harrison (1993), *Monopsony – Antitrust Law and Economics*, Princeton: Princeton University Press.

Borghesani, W.H. Jr., P.L. de la Cruz and D.B. Berry (1997), 'Food for thought: the emergence of power buyers and its challenge to competition analysis', Washington DC: Keller and Heckman.

Bork, R. (1978), *The Antitrust Paradox*, New York: Basic Books.

Bowley, A.L. (1928), 'Bilateral monopoly', *Economic Journal*, **38**, 651-9.

Bresnahan, T. and P. Reiss (1991), 'Entry and competition in concentrated markets', *Journal of Political Economy*, **99** (5), 977-1009.

Che, Y-K. and I. Gale (1997), 'Buyer alliances and managed competition', *Journal of Economics and Management Strategy*, **6**, 175-200.

C.I.R. (1998), *The European Retail Handbook*, 1998 edition, London: Corporate Intelligence on Retailing.

Clarke, R. (1985), *Industrial Economics*, Oxford: Basil Blackwell.

Clarke, R. and S.W. Davies (1982), 'Market structure and price-cost margins', *Economica*, **49**, 277-87.

Competition Commission (2000), 'Supermarkets: a report on the supply of groceries from multiple stores in the United Kingdom', London: HMSO.

Connor, J.M., R. Rogers and V. Bhagavan (1996), 'Concentration and countervailing power in the US food manufacturing industries', *Review of Industrial Organization*, **11**, 473-92.

Cruz, I., A. Fernandez and A. Rebello (1997), 'Estrategia de aplazamiento de pago en las empresas espanolas de distribucion de alimentacion', *Perspectivas del Sistema Financierio*, **57**, 45-57.

Davies, S.W., B.R. Lyons et al. (1996), *Industrial Organisation in the European Union*, Oxford University Press: Oxford.

Davies S.W., L. Rondi and A. Sembenelli (1998) 'SEM and the changing structure of EU manufacturing, 1987-93', University of East Anglia Economics Research Centre, Discussion Paper no. 9815.

Dobson, P.W. (1990), 'Vertically and horizontally related market structures', unpublished PhD thesis, University of London.

Dobson, P.W. (1998), 'The economic welfare implications of own label products', School of Management and Finance, Nottingham University, Discussion Paper 1998.IV.

Dobson, P.W. and M. Waterson (1996), *Vertical Restraints and Competition Policy*, Research Paper 12, London: Office of Fair Trading.

Dobson, P.W. and M. Waterson (1997), 'Countervailing power and consumer prices', *Economic Journal*, **107**, 418-30.

Dobson, P.W., M. Waterson and A. Chu (1998), *The Welfare Consequences of the Exercise of Buyer Power*, Research Paper 16, London: Office of Fair Trading.

Ehlermann, C.D. and L.L. Laudati (eds) (1997), *Proceedings of the European Competition Forum*, New York: John Wiley & Sons.

European Commission (1997a), *Green Paper on Vertical Restraints in EC Competition Policy*, Brussels: COM (96) 721 Final.

European Commission (1997b), *Commission Notice on the Definition of the Relevant Market for the Purposes of Community Law*, Brussels: OJ C 372.

Fellner, W. (1949), *Competition Among the Few*, New York: Knopf.

Forchheimer, K. (1908), 'Theoretisches zum unvollstandigen monopole', *Schmollers Jahrbuch*, 1-12.

Galbraith, J.K. (1952), *American Capitalism: The Concept of Countervailing Power*, Boston, MA: Houghton Mifflin.

Hannah, L. and J.A. Kay (1977), *Concentration in Modern Industry*, London: Macmillan.

Jacobson, J.M. and G.J. Dorman (1991), 'Joint purchasing, monopsony and antitrust', *Antitrust Bulletin*, **36**, 1-79.

Jacobson, J.M. and G.J. Dorman (1992), 'Monopsony revisited: a comment on Blair and Harrison', *Antitrust Bulletin*, **37**, 151-70.

Lerner, A.P. (1934), 'The concept of monopoly and the measurement of monopoly power', *Review of Economic Studies*, **1**, 157-75.

London Economics (1995), 'The retail grocery revolution', London.

Mathewson, G.F. and R.A. Winter (1996), 'Buyer groups', *International Journal of Industrial Organization*, **15**, 137-64.

Monopolies and Mergers Commission (1981), *Discounts to Retailers*, London: HMSO.

Morgan, E.J. (1994), 'European Community merger control in the service industries', *Service Industries Journal*, **14**, 62-84.

Morgan, E.J. (1997), 'European Community merger policy in the service industries: the second phase,' *Service Industries Journal*, **17**, 626-51.

Morgan, J.N. (1949), 'Bilateral monopoly and the competitive output', *Quarterly Journal of Economics*, **63**, 371-91.

Nichol, A.J. (1943), 'Review of a theoretical analysis of imperfect competition with special application to the agricultural industries by W.H. Nicholls', *Journal of Political Economy*, **51**, 82-84.

OECD (1981), 'Buying power: the exercise of market power by dominant buyers', Report of the Committee of Experts on Restrictive Business Practices, Paris.

OECD (1998), 'Buyer power of large scale multiproduct retailers', Background paper by the Secretariat, Roundtable on Buying Power, OECD, Paris.

Office of Fair Trading (1985), *Competition and Retailing*, London: HMSO.

Ratliff, J. (1998), 'Coming themes in EC vertical restraints', presented to the IBC Conference on European Competition Law, London.

Robinson, T. and C.M. Clarke-Hill (1995), 'International alliances in European retailing', in P.J. McGoldrick and G. Davies, *International Retailing Trends and Strategies*, London: Pitman Publishing.

Rubinstein, A. (1982), 'Perfect equilibrium in a bargaining model', *Econometrica*, **50**, 97-109.

Saving, T. (1970), 'Concentration ratios and the degree of monopoly', *International Economic Review*, **11**, 139-46.

Scherer, F.M. and D. Ross (1990), *Industrial Market Structure and Economic Performance*, Boston: Houghton Mifflin.

Shea, J. (1993), 'Do supply curves slope up?', *Quarterly Journal of Economics*, **108**, 1-32.

Stackelberg, H. von (1934), *Marktform und Gleichgewicht*, Berlin: Julius Springer.

Sutton, J. (1991), *Sunk Costs and Market Structure*, Boston: MIT Press.

Tordjman, A. (1994), 'European retailing: convergence, differences and perspectives', *International Journal of Retail and Distribution Management*, **22** (5), 3-19.

Veendorp, E.C.H. (1987), 'Oligoemporistic competition and the countervailing power hypothesis', *Canadian Journal of Economics*, **20**, 519-26.

Vogel, L. (1998), 'Competition law and buying power: the case for a new approach in Europe', *European Competition Law Review*, **1**, 4-11.

Williamson, O.E. (1968), 'Economics as an antitrust defense: the welfare tradeoffs', *American Economic Review*, **58**, 18-36.

Index